WHAT IF THERE WERE NO WHITES IN SOUTH AFRICA?

D1499114

WHAT IF THERE WERE
NO WHITES IN SOUTH AFRICA?

Ferial Haffajee

PICADOR AFRICA

First published in 2015 by Picador Africa
an imprint of Pan Macmillan South Africa
Private Bag X19, Northlands
Johannesburg, 2116

www.panmacmillan.co.za

ISBN 978-1-77010-440-2
eBook ISBN 978-1-77010-441-9

*The views and opinions expressed in the text that follows do not
necessarily reflect those of the publisher. Care has been taken
to ensure the accuracy of the facts and figures used, but any
corrections will be welcomed by the author and publisher, and
implemented in the event of a reprint.*

Editing by Sally Hines
Proofreading by Sean Fraser
Graphs and diagrams adapted by MDesign
Design and typesetting by Triple M Design, Johannesburg
Cover design by K4
Author photograph Gallo Images/*Destiny*/Nick Boulton

Printed and bound by Paarl Media Paarl

To my mother,
who has taught me the invaluable gratitude
of counting small blessings.

To City Press *and Media24*
for teaching me all I needed to know.
And more.

CONTENTS

PREFACE

My dear uncle, Mac Carim, was instrumental in making me see South Africa differently and not only through my jaundiced journalist's eyes, looking out only for what's wrong and not what's right. Early on in my editing stint at the *Mail & Guardian*, he said, 'Jeez, Fer, sometimes it's a wrist-slitter', in reference to various editions. So, now he's expecting this book, and said, 'What an interesting question!', when he saw the title.

Sorry, Uncle Mac, this book doesn't answer the question, 'What if whites hadn't colonised South Africa?' I intend to become an historian some day, but this is more a work of contemporary study – and then only of our freedom years.

I guess there are some who might answer my question this way: 'If there were no whites, this bloody country would go down the drain.' It's not that book either. Thankfully. And still others might answer, 'And it wouldn't be a moment too soon.' It's not that book either.

I prefer to think of this as a love song to an Mzansi I love dearly and as an attempt to see the possible.

1

WHAT IF THERE WERE NO WHITES?

I am controlled by a white guy.

Golden, when I look at him properly. Mishka. A gangly, golden Labrador who tries to tell me what to do from the morning to the night.

Beyond him, my complexes about racial superiority and inferiority have left the building – it has taken years and the arrival of freedom for that to happen. Perhaps because I grew up reporting the making of the Constitution and now enjoy the opportunities and protections of that sacrament, I feel my equality in deep and appreciative ways. Equality is a pillar of our Constitution and after having grown up feeling like a child of a lesser god, equality is a living concept for me.

wow

Of course, I am infuriated by former and unreconstructed privilege. I had been reading on invisibility. Then I went to the movies.

I was asking the manager something when a woman came straight up and proceeded to tell him about blocked toilets. No excuse me, no nothing. I objected, because that is what growing self-esteem does to you.

'I'm talking to him,' I said.

Like my experience in the Airport ' (handwritten marginal note)

The lady looked at me as if I'd dropped from Mars. 'What's your problem? You're so rude.'

I wasn't rude; I'd merely stepped out of the role she had planned for me and in doing so I upset the pecking order she had grown up with. I was invisible to her except, possibly, in servile roles she had come to expect of people like me.

——

I am 34 years old and about to get my dream job. Always a little in love with the *Mail & Guardian*, I have returned to it again and again like a homing pigeon in my first 15 years as a journalist. Now the editorship is up for grabs and I'm the front-runner. The feeling of a bubble bursting for me is hearing that two colleagues have put together a last-minute bid to get the deputy to apply late for the position.

Competition is positive but their rationale is not good. That I do not have the gumption to stand up to power. Why? There is nothing in my working history or my published work to give that idea. The perception is grounded in what I am. Black. A woman. Like the woman at the movies, they had a space for me in the hierarchy of what it took to be brave and to be an editor. Being black, being a woman wasn't in that space.

My neighbour in Parkhurst rings the intercom. 'Hi, is Muriel there?' Five years on and I am 'Muriel'. I sigh. I've given up. I've worked at it, dropping notes, dropping cakes, saying hi. Where I come from, neighbours know each other's stories and lives.

This suburban culture feels impenetrable sometimes. Surely he should know my name by now? I figure that I do not feature in my neighbour's frame of reference and so even my name is a fold of the tongue too far.

There's a television producer I've long admired for her crisp programming. We move in similar circles, but every time we meet she asks, 'What's your name again?' And then she looks me up and down and declares me more glamorous than she thought. Years ago, this may have hurt; now I put it down to early senility and move on.

I could fill a tome with the invisibility and slights and hurts of living in a racialised society. It would be easy. They happen often and they are remarkable every time. But years ago, I learnt to be honest with myself for that is not my whole life. This is. I am the fortunate black woman. Born poor but hefted into the middle class by a combination of the arrival of freedom and its attendant policies to make right a fractured past. This comes at the right moment for me.

I feel freedom. Breathe it. Speak it. Enjoy it. I know it only because I know its opposite. Apartheid, in all its social, political and economic dimensions, imprisoned me.

It cauterised dreams and terrorised us as my parents moved us from home to home to escape a hardening Group Areas Act. It broke up my extended family, some of whom went into self-imposed exile and others who left because South Africa under apartheid felt like a dead end. Every time I dreamt things as a curious child, it felt like the various manifestations of a cruel system conjoined to frustrate these dreams. It is what apartheid did

3

to my dreams that makes me most zealous about my freedom. And it is probably what has prodded this book.

And so, I breathe freedom. I like living here and now, though I know and report freedom's limitations every day. In terms of our freedom, we are governed by a black majority. Power has changed hands and with it all the associated levers of fiscal and sociological influence. At national, provincial and local level, the images of governing authority are black.

My tax no longer goes to an illegitimate regime but to a black state that uses it to redistribute, in the main, to people who were not as fortunate as I was when freedom came. Policy is determined by black people – my life is run by a democratically elected black government, and so is yours. It has been this way for over 20 years and my sense is black people are in office and in power.

This is true culturally, too. I live in a black country from Cape Point to Musina. I feel this as much as I did when I travelled to newly freed Harare as a kid and understood what freedom would feel like one day. That day has come for me. It does not feel contested; it feels altered by our recent history. Or 'transformed' in the original way the word was meant and not in the contortions we now apply to its original and positive meaning. The dominant culture has altered. Blackness is in the music that tinkles across the radio stations I tune in to, the websites I surf, the Twitter timelines I follow.

From the lyricism of Lira to the challenging sound of Nakhane Touré, I cannot honestly claim that my world has not changed – that it remains a Eurocentric enclave in a black continent. No.

Black ownership and blackness is in the literature, in a body of work that has been the interpreter and healer of my maladies on the road from broken to free. It is in the soapies, in the diverse worlds they depict. In *Isidingo*. *Muvhango*. It is in the movies I take out of my local video shop. *Gangster's Paradise: Jerusalema*. *Fanie Fourie's Lobola*.

It is in fashion: in the texture of the cloth, the cut of the fabric, the rub of Kente against Dutch Wax print.

In my world, in yours, can we truly claim it to be otherwise? Everywhere I turn, a generation born free is in chains. Everywhere I turn, a generation born free is talking as if it is at once obsessed by and imprisoned by whiteness and white supremacy. The black obsession with whiteness and white privilege is all, it seems, we ever talk about in sustained ways in our national conversations. To my ear it sounds as if whites are spoken of as if they are a majority in power, rather than a small group of varied political sentiments, but one that largely supports the Democratic Alliance.

At first, I think it is a minor belief that whites still control culture and thought. But as I explore, it feels generational – as if it is the discourse of a new generation. And, increasingly, it is also that of an older generation that has revised its position on non-racialism and replaced it with a simmering resentment about a perceived white cultural and financial domination that has replaced formal apartheid.

Can it be? It can't. The simple facts don't allow it. The narrative feels like it is borrowed straight from the United States and it is laced with the language of an oppressed minority in the claws of a powerful majority. So, rather than understanding and analysing whites as a formerly advantaged ruling elite, the South African narrative sounds as if whites are a majority (or at least equivalent in number to black people).

There are a diminishing number of whites in South Africa but the current discourse makes it seem as if they are a much larger part of the population. Whenever I ask groups of black people to estimate the number of whites in South Africa their answer is inevitably an over-estimation. When I try to tease out why this is, people say it is because whites exercise an economic and cultural power so significant that it is overpowering.

The reasons black people still adopt the narrative of a minority in opposition to a majority are manifold. To stand where Martin Luther King stood at the Lincoln Memorial to declare his dream is to understand the compelling character of the American civil rights movement. And the role of African Americans in South Africa's final years of struggle is significant.

As scholars, thinkers and journalists jetted to the United States to study, they imported the culture of the black American struggle for rights back into South Africa. You wouldn't know if you landed from an extraterrestrial place that whites in South Africa are a relatively small minority. Each national census reveals the number of whites here is in steady decline.

This majority believing it is a minority cascades into a pool of problems. We underestimate black progress all the time – egged on by political leaders who use race as a neat deflection from the failing of the state.

I do not for a moment suggest we are transformed from what we were into what we should be. But the numbers are persuasive.

We have not stood still. Research by Futurefact shows phenomenal and rapid social mobility in South Africa: the numbers of people who self-identified as having moved up the class ladder in comparison with their parents shows significant growth.

Black people like me, a largely first-generation middle class, have buoyed the economy. With no assets, a black middle class has bought homes and filled them, and filled the homes of extended families; a black middle class has driven cars off showroom floors and has ballooned the fortunes of the life and pensions industry by buying millions of unit trusts, endowment and funeral policies, life insurance and retirement funds. There is a generation of black farmers tilling the land and thumbing their noses at the architects of the 1913 Land Act. The numbers are small but nowhere near as small as the figure of 5% that I've heard bandied about.

Why are we like this? Why are we unable to see meaningful transformation or unwilling to see it? For most of my writing life, I have tracked the changes. They started years ago.

I arrive at the *Financial Mail* in 1999. It is an august and elegant newsroom and I am very excited to be there. I get an office with my name on the door. The *FM* allows me autonomy and space and I get invitations to lunch. For a girl from Bosmont who grew up on chip rolls on pavements as lunch, I love it.

And I hate it. The *FM* is also stuffily traditional and deeply unreconstructed.

The *FM*, as it was at the time, was rich and sure of its place in the world. Its pages were the authoritative guide to corporate South Africa. And the picture was odd. It was as if political power had changed but not corporate power, and neither had the magazine caught up with what change means.

Although this was 1999, all the columnists were white and most of them were white men. There was a Tuesday conference where, I observe for months, nobody says anything about what increasingly feels like a media injustice to me. So, one day, I pipe up: 'When will we have some black columnists? I count seven written by white men. One by a white woman.'

You can hear the pin drop. The shift of discomfort is palpable. My heart's beating as hearts do when they confront uncomfortable hegemonies anywhere. The progressives mutter about not being able to find any. The conservatives glower.

Being a practical Haffajee girl, I decide to do something about my angst. A colleague, William Mervin Gumede, and I publish the first *Little Black Book* to bridge the chasm between the worlds and ensure my colleagues can't say they can't find any black columnists.

And so, through the next years, we publish *The Little Black Book*. It covers all major sectors and includes the public and non-profit sector. Every year it gets fatter and fatter. Advertising in it is good. Margins are excellent. The columns in the *FM* change. Barney Mthombothi hones the style that will make him South Africa's most symphonic columnist. Over the next 17 years it becomes part of my practice to track people for whom the new South Africa is a Mecca.

The *Women's Book* follows, then the *200 Young South Africans You Must Take to Lunch*, then the *100 World Class South Africans* at *City Press*. These compendiums are filled to the brim with people for whom freedom is a tangible good.

The years of burrowing through reams of research reveal a depth of talent and of transformation. There isn't a sector where black aspiration and talent don't meet in wonderful harmony to reshape how we understand ourselves. From the arts to mining; from financial services to fashion; from universities to the Union Buildings, I found real black and female leadership. At the *Mail & Guardian*, the publication of a new generation of young people we think are influential is the proudest work I've ever edited for it is a genuine showcase of a full range of young South Africans who have grasped freedom by the wings and flown with it.

So why do we find ourselves here? When I preach my gospel of change, of black accomplishment and of the good and healthy fruits of freedom, it is as if I am the anti-Christ. It is as if I have journeyed to a place where nothing has changed, where an oppressive minority controls thought and destiny. A place where black people labour under a system of white supremacy.

Do I live in a different world? Am I crazy? As I research, I see our debates, our racialised world view is built in a world where the black and white middle class play bumper cars. It is a rivalry for how history is understood and weighted. It is a rivalry about whose culture will rule the roost.

It wasn't supposed to be this way.

———

I know things have changed, but as I stand and survey in 2015, I see they haven't changed sufficiently after two decades. And the pattern in workplaces is the same. It is the cappuccino – mixed to a good brown at the bottom, a layer of thick white froth and sprinkles of chocolate. The impetus for change I tracked at the start of the century has slowed. I speak to boardrooms fairly often. And, yes, if they are not in sectors with high regulation (mining, telecoms) or owned and part-owned by the state, the grooves worn by our past have not changed sufficiently.

By the end of 2013, about one in five top managers was black; for senior managers it was one in four. In both categories, even if you group black, coloured and Indian people together, there are far more white people (the majority of whom are men) running corporate South Africa.

This is huge for it means that in the entire world of work outside of the state sector, the patterns of old remain intact. The leaders and the led have not changed substantially enough to re-sculpt how either of these two positions in society and in work is understood. Good societies have healthy mixes in both parts of this equation. In a diverse country like ours, the proportions have to be inverted to alter workplace culture and instil black leadership as the norm rather than the exception.

For the purposes of research, I turn my white privilege antenna back on. I realise that somewhere along the way, I have grown oblivious to its irritations. 'White privilege' refers to a set of behaviours that underlie conduct that inflames South Africa's sometimes awful race relations – it is often unconscious, the mark of a former ruling class. Having turned it on, I can't wait to turn it back off.

Zelda la Grange's set of exasperated tweets in January 2015 do deep damage because she is regarded as a figure of national solidarity with black struggles. Yet her tweet bomb reveals her loyalties to be split between here and France – she is of French Huguenot stock and in one of her tweets she plans to ask French leader François Hollande for citizenship. In another, she suggests that Oom Jan (van Riebeeck) should not have set foot here.

But white privilege can also be seen at the annual office party and what is planned for it. Which culture is dominant? White privilege screams its anger in a sustained narrative against employment equity and black empowerment – as if it does not realise that anything but an economy owned in proportion to the demographics of South Africa is anti-democratic.

Of course, you will find black non-executive directors and senior managers in the boardrooms but the proportions are inverted here – blacks a minority and whites a majority. While we don't change workplaces, the corrosive debates about race in South Africa will get worse.

It is in workplaces where racial bumper cars play out and crash into wider society, bringing all their pains with them. It is here that impatient black aspiration meets dogged white self-protection, where our pain lies and where leadership does not lie. The annual Reconciliation Barometer of the Institute for Justice and Reconciliation reveals this – generationally, South Africans are mixing less.

Levels of socialisation, and the development of stronger

relationships across race lines, are consistently lower in successive survey rounds. In 2012, 17.8% of South Africans always or often socialise with people of other races, for example, in their homes, or in the homes of friends. A further 21.6% do so sometimes, and more than half (56.6%) rarely or never socialise across race lines. Whites and Indian/Asian youth are more likely to indicate a strong association with others of the same race or economic class than adults and, across the board, socialisation across race is much more common among younger people than older ones.

DISAPPROVAL OF RACIAL INTEGRATION BY AGE AND RACE, 2012 (%)						
Disapproval		**White**	**Indian/Asian**	**Coloured**	**Black**	**Total**
Living in an integrated neighbourhood	Youth	21.9	15.4	15.7	18.6	18.5
	Adults	21.3	6.4	11.2	18.3	17.6
	Total	21.5	9.6	13.1	18.5	18.1
Working for someone of another race	Youth	9.6	8.0	29.9	20.2	20.2
	Adults	26.4	15.0	27.6	19.0	20.4
	Total	21.4	12.5	28.6	19.6	20.3
Close relative marries someone of another race	Youth	42.7	34.7	17.3	23.5	24.1
	Adults	30.2	21.4	21.6	25.5	25.5
	Total	34.0	26.2	19.8	24.5	24.8
Integrated schools	Youth	7.7	0.0	7.6	16.0	14.9
	Adults	12.9	7.5	8.3	14.9	13.9
	Total	11.4	4.8	8.0	15.5	14.4

I don't want to ... live with ... work with ... marry and go to school with ...

Source: The South African Reconciliation Barometer: 2011–2014; Institute for Justice and Reconciliation.

The place of greatest racial interaction is the workplace or the university or social media where the middle classes meet and where we decide what we will be. It is here where non-racialism has come to die. If we let it.

—

what does non-racialism mean?

It is a sunny Monday in summer 2015 at the Wits Club in Johannesburg. The trees throw warm shadows. I sit, nervous as hell, about to stage an argument for non-racialism and a defence of the media's role in covering race. It will be a tough afternoon – how tough I don't realise. It is an exciting panel. John Perlman. Xolela Mangcu. Eusebius McKaiser. And me. Quickly, it goes completely off-topic, becoming an impassioned panel about race in South Africa 21 years after apartheid formally ended. I realise it didn't.

The place where I learnt most of what I know about non-racialism – this University of the Witwatersrand – eschews it as an ephemeral and dated dream. Or the brain trust does at least. Each one of this august panel reflects a highly racialised world in which whiteness, rather than non-racialism, is the dominant ideology. Each speaker is brilliant and forensic in unpacking how racial consciousness has come to congeal and frustrate the rainbow nation.

Whiteness is the study of a system of privilege in which white people are held to be at the centre of gaze. It is, I find, an ideology and school of thought that has come to surpass non-racialism

13

as a prism through which to understand contemporary South Africa. At the panel, I hear for the first time the extension of whiteness into an understanding of our country as functioning under a system of 'white supremacy'. I think I am hearing wrong when Osiame Molefe voices the concept during question time at the panel. I am amazed when a substantial part of the room nods in agreement to an assertion that a supremacist ideology is still in place. I feel, not for the first time, as if I live in a different country with a narrative I find hard to recognise.

Supremacy implies a system of ownership of culture and practice and a dominion over another. But my perception is that I live in a black majority country where there is a healthy diversity of views and interests. Of course we have work to do. Lots of it. But I am astounded that so many of our country's men and women can feel oppressed enough to still feel a supremacist setting that characterises South Africa. What has happened? As a child of freedom, I feel my country offers a life sketched with many and varied opportunities – clearly, it is not a universalised sketch. And, so, this work is my effort to find out why not.

———

What if there were no whites? The economy would either tank or be more equitably owned. That depends on global forces often beyond national control. Wealth has neither been substantially redistributed nor grown to change its structure sufficiently. Of course there is change. The numbers of black and white middle-class people are, according to some measures, equal and, in other surveys, blacks now outnumber whites. This is hugely significant, but it is insufficient. The popular narrative that seems to believe whites possess so much wealth that its redistribution would in one fell swoop deal with black poverty and unemployment is at odds with reality.

If white wealth were nationalised, the size of the black elite would swell slightly, but the overall impact would be economically negligible. In fact, the numbers obtained through the 2011 census show that if you take all white resources (from wealth and education to housing, toilets and water) and distribute them to black South Africans, it would hardly move the needle on national development.

To give two examples. According to the 2011 census, over 4 million black South Africans are not attending an educational institution at their relevant level. If the total number of white South Africans at every educational level, which is just shy of 800 000 people, was removed from the picture, it would take care of only 19% of the problem. Over 80%, or 3.3 million, of the original number of black South Africans would still not be attending an educational institution. And when it comes to water, out of 1.6 million white-headed households at the time of the 2011 census, over 1.5 million had access to piped water within their homes. Out of the 11.3 million black-headed households, 3.9 million had the same access. So if all the whites left, it would make room for just over 20% of blacks who do not have this service. The rest of the 80% – about 5.9 million people – would still have inferior access to piped water.

Non-racialism is so abused I can see why it has lost credibility. It has become the easy slogan of the citizen who doesn't want to engage in hard work. So, you can read a thousand examples of people who allege employment equity is wrong because it is against non-racialism. If called out on a blatant exhibition of white privilege, sloganists will claim it is against non-racialism.

I found an effort to boycott Woolworths a few years ago breathtakingly naive. Woolworths came under social media fire because a set of advertisements had declared its commitment to employment equity. That set the bulldogs of the anti-equity lobby on the retailer. Twitter and Facebook were ablaze with impassioned white privilege masquerading as an army of defenders of non-racialism. Talk about losing the plot. Non-racialism, as a constitutional principle and an organising political practice, has never meant not seeing race. It is a philosophy that acknowledges the role of race in constructing the country, economy and social relations, and then actively sets out to dismantle these relationships to eventually see and commune with each other beyond our racial identities. We are currently as far from it as we are from the moon – but the principle should be resurrected for it is our founding constitutional value.

———

It is one of those ice-blue winter days on the highveld in the late 1980s. I bring my own brown bread lunch to a youth congress meeting at Wits because I have no money to buy an alternative.

At lunch, all the students and activists who are there scrape their money together. We eat together – black, white, coloured and Indian, it doesn't matter who contributed and who did not. Coming, as I did, from the coloured group area of Bosmont, university was my first experience of working across race lines for a common purpose.

In student socialist organisations, it was the same reaching across the racial prisons apartheid had set up for us. In Mayfair, I worked with movements seeking to end Group Areas Act evictions. Again, we worked across class and racial lines. On Wednesday evenings, while at university, I would walk around the corner to a state school where we had use of a classroom and taught the area's domestic workers and security guards to write their names and to sign their signatures; to master simple maths. I realise, now, what a privilege this work was because it was an outcome of planned non-racialism where people worked together across class and race lines for the ends of social justice.

Non-racial struggles for justice always saw race, but understood that we have to move beyond race, ethnicity and tribe to construct a human consciousness and a national consciousness. Somewhere in the past 21 years, we lost the meaning and purpose of non-racialism and it has congealed into a nasty race consciousness.

What if there were no whites? And blacks? And coloureds and Indians? Besides these constituent parts of us, there were also 280 454 people called 'other' in the most recent census – I guess permanent residents. We are here on this beautiful, troubled corner of southern Africa and none of us can be wished away. It is our simple truth.

———

So, how many whites do you think live in South Africa?

I suspect if you asked the majority of South Africans, they would not know the answer. Black South Africans, I think, believe there are far higher numbers of whites in South Africa than the statistics show. Cultural and economic power amplify the power of whites, who, in reality, are a tiny and diminishing part of the South African population landscape. In 1996, whites comprised 10.9% of the population. In 2014, Statistics South Africa's projections put the percentage at 8.4% – indicating that, as a proportion of the total, the group is smaller. In 1996, black African people comprised 76.7% of the population; the 2014 projection placed the majority at 80.2%.

Yet, the debate and tenor of discussion in South Africa presents blacks and whites as comprising equal numbers, where, if the power of one is transferred to the other, the panacea would be found. My thesis is not to diminish or compact the equality or voice of white South Africans, but to highlight a narrative I find both interesting and disturbing; it is a false consciousness constructed out of our past.

The allied trend that complements this narrative is one of identification. South Africa now has a substantial black middle class and a smaller but powerful elite.

Given Mkhari is the most powerful black media owner in South Africa. In addition to film companies, he owns a fleet of radio stations, the most prominent of which is Power FM in Gauteng. Recently, his tweet helped me to expand my theory. He said, 'We cannot rest until black poverty falls.'

The idea of black poverty is always presented as the outcome of white wealth, but what South Africa has is a poverty problem, not necessarily a black poverty problem because it is a largely black country. It might sound facetious given the racial wealth gap, but unless we begin to understand poverty and unemployment as South African problems, not racialised issues only, then it allows scapegoating and a rhetoric that fails to substantially tackle the policy and efficiency measures needed now.

I've asked roomfuls of black middle-class South Africans which class they are from and the answer is inevitably 'peasant' or 'working class' – dependent usually on whether their family is rural or urban.

The reason for this answer is the struggle against apartheid. Built upon a Marxist analysis of society, most people I know will assign themselves to a category at the lower level of society, even if they are black middle class with property, assets and income as well as a lifestyle that is decidedly what once would have been called bourgeois. At its heart is a social solidarity that runs deep: you cannot identify separately from community, society and family, and to declare yourself a class above would be to do precisely that.

People don't identify differently because it creates more categories of separation, which run counter to the deep links of community that lie at the heart of South Africa.

Even if your life is global and elite and your style is too, your self-identification will, largely, remain linked to the black experience of being in poverty. Social solidarity is good. It will ensure that the left-behind in South Africa are not rendered invisible to remain left behind in the way that, say, India's under-classes are. The corollary, however, is that the developmental path ahead is often perceived to be that the solution to black poverty lies in white wealth.

Any of the range of opinion writers or analysts amplify this narrative that the wealth gap is only racial and that if whites did *something*, then black poverty would be resolved. I've asked and read widely, but I've yet to understand what this *something* is. It is built on shifting terrain: most often it is expressed as support for a wealth tax. Or redistribution. In corporate circles, it is usually a lobby for black empowerment charters. At its heart is the population myth that builds black and white as equal in number or, in extreme cases, it takes the language of black South Africans being a minority like black Americans.

The struggle against apartheid was profoundly impacted by the American civil rights movement. The links of solidarity between black Americans such as Andrew Young and Jesse Jackson influenced South Africa's struggle in language, culture and style. Black American solidarity was a vital cog in finally dislodging apartheid as the sanctions movement isolated this regime.

But a side effect of the twinning of the two struggles meant the political language and understanding was also assimilated. During the struggle, this was fine as the apartheid state had and exercised behemoth power. Twenty-one years on, it has left a mark that is less salubrious. While black Americans are a minority, black South Africans are a majority whose influencers and political leaders project it as a minority. Today the currency of white supremacy as an explanation of South African society is gaining, not losing, traction. If you ask what this white supremacy is, its proponents will point to the difficulties in workplaces where power has not shifted into more fair or representative forms or, otherwise, it is proxy for a capitalist market economy.

The trouble with a narrative that believes South Africa comprises equal numbers of blacks and whites is that it is profoundly disempowering for blacks as it sets whites up as far more dominant than a relatively small minority with post-colonial privilege.

And its creates a false expectation that sets its store in wealth redistribution rather than in wealth creation as the path we need to embark on to secure better black lives. But the ruling class is no longer white; it is demonstrably black.

I cannot say with honesty that the people who run my life in any sphere are white. At work, it's a mixed bag (though I like to think each of us is our own boss). My city is run by a black mayor. My province by a black premier. My country by a black president. With their hands on the levers of various public fiscus, it cannot possibly be that blacks are in office, but not in power.

Even if all white wealth was taken tomorrow and distributed to black South Africans, it wouldn't go far. It's simple maths. The narrative also ignores a crucial ratio. By some counts, the number of black middle-class people now outstrip the number of white middle-class people. This is a phenomenal fruit of freedom and success of a range of democratic-era policies, but it is not owned, either by the influencers of society or by the political class. At least at its middle, black people have caught up with and outpaced their white counterparts.

The 2014 Reconciliation Barometer points to some interesting perceptions around economic justice and reconciliation. In general, the majority of South Africans describe themselves as 'poor' or 'struggling to get by' and class/income is seen as the biggest source of division and impediment to reconciliation. While all South Africans share a similar desire to forgive the injustices of the past and move forward, white South Africans are 20–30% less likely to agree with the need to continue to support victims of apartheid or that economic redress is required for reconciliation.

A particularly pronounced split is evident in response to a question that assesses apartheid's economic legacy: whether or not black South Africans are still poor today as a result of the lasting effects of apartheid. Eighty-two per cent of black South Africans agree; 73% of Indian/Asians; 61.4% of coloured people; and only about 50.6% of whites agree. Add to this the fact that only 33% of white, Indian and coloured young people, on average, feel that economic justice and greater equality are necessary preconditions for reconciliation, and you set the stage for differing perceptions and priorities.

———

For me, creating 'the good society' requires doubling the size of the middle class in South Africa and keeping the top and bottom

of society smaller. But this demands a difficult set of policy measures that place employment (and not job protection or high
minimum wages) at the centre of the labour market debate.

It also requires delinking from the racial understanding of how
wealth is grown. And for the voluble white rights movement, it
demands acknowledging that employment equity worked and
that we need more not less of it before we can kiss it goodbye
with a sunset clause. In white society, there is natter that most
personal taxes are paid by whites. It comes up quite regularly
when I talk about the public good impact of extending a social
grant to 16.4 million South Africans, which is a crocheted mix of
old-age pensions, child grants, as well as foster and dependency
grants.

There is a social media meme being spread by the white right,
which equates almost all personal taxpayers as being white. It
is a myth as the personal income tax burden is held equally by
black and white South Africans. VAT is a shared burden. Perhaps
whites also do not understand themselves to be a relatively small
part of the South African matrix of people and demand special
rights and privileges.

The wealth tax is a popular and populist call made regularly
by sectors that include churches and civil society, and occasionally in political life, too. But, in reality, South Africa's tax system
cannot be more progressive. At the top ends of the income scale,
tax rates are decidedly Scandinavian. The marginal rate kicks in
when you earn in the region of R6 200.00 per month, meaning
the lower working class pays no tax.

Eradicating black poverty lies in the hands of black people, not of white people. It is the cost and gift of being a black leader. Black hands hold all the levers of encouraging wealth creation and of ensuring the private sector gears a growth path that gifts more black people with opportunity and ownership. You wouldn't say it if you observe our narrative, but it is true. And not to acknowledge this truth or to allow a myth of equal populations to exist does not serve the common purpose.

———

The Johannesburg Stock Exchange (JSE) is built high. It looms over the street in Sandton where it is based, its glass-and-granite exterior extolling money and power. It's an easy target. In 2011, then African National Congress (ANC) Youth League president Julius Malema pulled off a tour de force. He called a march of jobless youth that started at the JSE and ended in Pretoria. His followers marched for almost an entire night. The JSE hulked over the gathered youth on the pavement – impenetrable, like the world of wealth is for two to three million young compatriots who have no work or opportunity.

The JSE has become a symbol of the market, but it can be used inaccurately to portray a picture of less new wealth than has been created. What does a troubled president do when faced with the meme #PayBackTheMoney? He begins a money myth. And, so, early one morning, President Jacob Zuma started the 3% story. He said black people owned only 3% of the JSE. The power of that statement lies in what is not said and what is assumed. And that is that white people therefore own 97% of the JSE.

The statement went viral and it has spiralled into 'truth'. But it's not. When the JSE still called the diamond building at Johannesburg's west end home, the former *Weekly Mail*, my first employer, decided it needed to nod at business coverage and so I found myself working for the business team. That was a hyperbole for the esteemed Reg Rumney and the one trainee assigned to him. I was that one. He dispatched me to the JSE and said I needed to do something on socially responsible investment.

It was a bewildering place. Before online trading and settlement, it still had a trading floor – of largely white men. I was to meet one of them. David Shapiro is my favourite trader until today because he agreed to an interview and didn't throw me out on the grounds of ignorance. Instead, he took in my red jeans, takkies and Che Guevara T-shirt and said I looked like a *Weekly Mail* journalist. Nothing has ever made me prouder. Like most radical youth and people of a leftist persuasion, to me the JSE was the symbol of 'the market' – that beast that kept apartheid rolling, the heart of capitalism. Shapiro's lesson was one all South Africans should learn: all of us are part-owners of the JSE – or we are if we hold unit trusts, retirement annuities, pension funds or share incentives.

Yet many South Africans remain as ignorant of this as I was back then with my red jeans. And so President Zuma's statement has built a head of steam and been repeated into a social truth. Yet the take-up of investment instruments by black people in just over two decades of freedom and opportunity has been nothing short of phenomenal.

———

When my dad died, I sorted through his papers and got waylaid and damp-eyed by his notes, his meticulous spending lists and his newspaper cuttings of my worst first pieces of journalism. In among his goods were lots of dog-eared lists of permutations of numbers to win the Lotto. Until his dying month, my dad made these lists, convinced that he would crack it.

We laughed (and I think my mum cried) at how he applied his beautiful mathematical mind to this end. My father was clever: he could add lines of figures effortlessly, a skill that made him useful to a succession of bosses in the rag trade who valued his loyalty and agility with numbers. He never got far and was shocked when retrenched mercilessly despite his loyalty when Chinese textiles and clothing flooded our shores once the economy opened. Thereafter life was more precarious and so when the Lotto arrived he was an early adopter. I've kept a few of my dad's long lines to remind me of him and to caution me not to get too comfortable in a market-based system. In among these, I found a single policy of my dad's. It paid out R10 000.00 – all my mum received by way of security. He left us a legacy of laughs, fun and a singular *joie de vivre*, but nothing by way of material goods.

I suspect it's the same for most of us first-generation, black, middle-class people. There are no policies, no trust funds, no inheritances and endowments at different life stages. There is no inheritance. No knowledge of or appreciation of how a market can be made to work as a tool of intergenerational wealth transfer because the JSE is where money goes to grow. Yet, I'd wager most of us who are employed are invested there.

I've shunned the Lotto to save. If David Shapiro taught me how an exchange works, then Tracy Davenport has shown how it can work for me. I don't think my factory-worker dad ever needed to fill in a tax return because his wage didn't require it, so my taxes were a mess. A friend recommended Tracy. She fixed those. And then Tracy taught me the tricks of being employed and middle class: how you need to care for every life stage; what you need to insure for and against; and how much you need to save to enjoy a decent lifestyle when you choose to stop working.

When this isn't taught as part of family smarts, it's a bewildering world of annuities and calculations. So statuesque Tracy with blonde, flowing locks is Amazonian for me. A self-made woman, she is South Africa's answer to the American middle-class's Suze Orman who preaches the mantra of saving over spending. Through Tracy, I've learnt the value of investing in well-managed unit trusts, which always outperform the market average and also earn more than an interest-bearing account in a low-inflation economy. My cousins and I are the first generation of our family to hold retirement policies. It grows every year, giving me a cushion my dad could only imagine and dream of in the lines of numbers of such promise in Lotto tickets.

I am an indirect shareholder in the JSE. You will not find me, or millions of first-generation investors like me, in the president's 3%, yet we are a tangible example of real empowerment. We are building assets that are being used to develop South Africa and to pass on to the next generation. If you take the broad-based definition of shareholding, black South Africans have done well to change the colour of wealth. Yet President Zuma and other senior political leaders and empowerment lobbyists actively seek to downgrade the experiences of people like me who now own as much as white indirect shareholders.

What does it mean for me? Agency, most of all. I have enough to live better than the hand-to-mouth existence I grew up on in a family that had only enough for the bare necessities and the odd holiday in Durban. In such a world, your horizons are shorted, your dreams curtailed. It also means independence – having your own money and investments cauterises the vein of dependence.

At the least, as I have mentioned above, there are roughly equal numbers of black and white middle-class South Africans. If I were a political leader, I'd be shouting it from the rooftops since we are a fruit of freedom. If it had not been for the planned and political project of black empowerment and employment equity, the workplace would have remained closed and protected for Boer cronies and a tight circle of concentrated Anglo-Saxon capital. If the state had not been transformed from apartheid's oppression to democracy's freedom, space would not have been made for a generation of entrepreneurs and employees who are changing the colour of money.

Is it happening fast enough? Of course not. Is it deep enough? Really meaningful change would lie in a critical mass at least triple the current rate of indirect holding in listed wealth because that would mean substantial growth in employment since it is generally the middle-class working population that can invest in a pension fund and short-term investments.

Why are we, indirect black shareholders, an uncomfortable truth for our president and for other political leaders? Is it because it's politically more savvy to present the story that blacks own 3% of the JSE and to leave lingering in the air the untruth that whites own 97% because you can crochet a political ideology of populism more easily around a statistic like this one?

It enables the creation of an amorphous other in 'whites' to keep an enemy that is easier to fight than crippling corruption, unemployment and a wealth gap that require deeper leadership than our political class is currently capable of.

2

POWER IS A DIFFICULT CLOAK
TO WEAR COMFORTABLY

As a labour and business journalist for the *Mail & Guardian* in the early 1990s, I would occasionally get dispatched to company results presentations or to hobnob with captains of industry. To tell you how we dressed, I'll reel forward from that time to when the immaculately attired Zimbabwean business person Trevor Ncube purchased the newspaper.

One of his first tasks, he said, was to change the attire. Shorts. Flip-flops. Takkies. Out. Jeans were only allowed if worn with a belt and if ironed. Chinos. Ironed. Shirts. No T-shirts. The *Mail & Guardian* staff was horrified. I had moved on but back then I wore jeans and political T-shirts. Trevor was trying to make the highbrow *Mail & Guardian* more establishment, but its decided anti-establishment perch gave me a good vantage point to learn about ruling power and ascendant challenges to that ruling power. We were the voice of that challenge.

My collision, thus dressed, with the Anglo-Saxon establishment is etched in my mind. I had been sent to attend an Anglo American cocktail party, possibly regarding its results presentation, as we were trying to make an effort to take business seriously.

I was, as they say on Twitter, *awks* (awkward) – out of my depth and out of place. It was stuffy and foreign. Dripping with wealth and dripping with ignorance about the country in which it made its eye-popping fortune. I was dressed differently to the assembled set of suits and I thought very differently to the journalists they knew. They were white. Pinstriped. The journalists were white. Suited.

An executive tried to chat to me – he chose the topic of cricket as there was a Test on. I volunteered that Test cricket was boring and that I preferred action cricket or limited overs. The man was horrified. We had no more to say to each other. I stayed for about 20 minutes; being anti-establishment was hard work when you slammed into the establishment.

So, I know an establishment, I know a white establishment, when I see one and my establishment is black. The anatomy of *my* country is black. My country, that is – the one I choose to live in.

I know South Africa is unreconstructed in parts where black people do not yet constitute the new establishment (and that is largely in the corporate private sector) but my experience is different.

The political establishment is decidedly black – the impact of democracy meant it would automatically be so. For me, the black political kingdom is very powerful. The governing ANC runs South Africa with a massive majority – it does not govern in a shaky coalition. The state is huge – its spending ability alone is at R500 billion a year. Armed with this spending and control over licences (gambling, telecommunications, financial services,

31

broadcasting), the state has massive say over the economy and polity.

My social and cultural establishment is decidedly black; all the cues and cultures I walk in are black. My opinions, beliefs, principles and values are derived from black South African experience and culture first and then from universal philosophies and practices.

When I go to corporate cocktail functions or to diplomatic affairs nowadays, I am no longer like a square peg in a round hole because the establishment has changed in its formative material to something I know and understand.

———

Brunswick is a leading global corporate communications company that works only at high levels in South Africa. Headed by Itumeleng Mahabane, in 2015 the company got Phumzile Mlambo-Ngcuka, the executive director of United Nations Women and a former deputy president of South Africa, to address its annual women's day breakfast.

She was wonderful and global – easily a future South African president if our politics was not so Machiavellian. Gathered around the breakfast tables was a who's who of female South African corporate life: vice presidents, chief operating officers, executive directors and heads of strategy. Diversity was healthy (at least half the women there were black) and a clear example of a new establishment that would not have been possible before freedom came along with the constitutional principle of non-sexism.

From this vantage point, I have watched the establishment thinking on race begin to change and move to a new establishment – a generational shift to new black opinion-makers has radicalised race discourse and began to question fundamentally the terms of the transition and the idea of non-racialism. It has interested me that, on the face of it, this new establishment had voice, agency, could pick its roles in society and was *the* power. So, what was eating at this new power that its discourse was so enraged with whites and so disempowered despite the end of white minority rule over two decades ago?

To write, I needed to understand, so I asked a range of South Africans who represent my new establishment why they do not feel this way themselves.

———

'What if there were no whites in South Africa?' I asked a series of people. Would it matter that much given that blacks hold a substantial majority in South Africa?

It turned out to be perceived as one of the most dumb-arsed questions possible – the truth of white power is held to be so self-evident. People I know are horrified at the asking of the question – as if it betrays a surprising naivety. As an editor, and a progressive one, I should know better.

My first port of call is Andile Mngxitama, the political

philosopher, activist, rebel and, until recently, member of parliament for the Economic Freedom Fighters (EFF).

Andile comments, 'I think it was the [political commentator] Aubrey Matshiqi who coined this thing of South Africa being a black majority which is a cultural minority. The real power holders in this country are white, knowledge holders are whites.'

I find variations of this idea everywhere: that blacks are in office, but not in power; that there has been a transfer of political power but not of economic power; that blacks are a majority in number only but hold the hegemony in almost no other sphere of South African life. Political power has not translated into any other kind of power, be it economic, social or cultural.

In many ways it feels to me as if black South Africans, and certainly the country's new generation of influencers, present themselves as a minority faced with an overwhelming and oppressive majority.

My other go-to thinker is Professor Melissa Steyn, who is director of the Wits Centre for Diversity Studies. She is a totemic figure in the popular study of whiteness. Studies of whiteness are aimed at threading a consciousness of white power, privilege and supremacy into their students and into society. Popularised in the United States, there is now a growing body of academics that use these studies to frame an understanding of race in South Africa.

Whites are no longer the power brokers, I suggest to Melissa, repeating my view that whites are a population of diminishing numbers and power and that their hold over South Africa is often imagined. Whiteness, I argue, places and holds whites at the centre of the national gaze when in fact the quest is for the realisation of socio-economic goals.

'Whoah! Not so fast,' is her key response.

'The two main ideological systems that have constructed the whole of the modern world [are] white supremacy and patriarchy. So there is actually no thinking ourselves out of this.

'These are globally dominating ideologies that have constructed the world as we know it and there is no easy route out of it. So I think one can't sort of flagellate black people for in some ways being trapped in this mindset or in these ideological structures because on the one hand whiteness is still a factor.

'You go somewhere like South Korea, or China, you try to buy skin creams that don't have lighteners in them, you'd hardly find them.

'And there are vaginal lightening creams, and God knows what all, and the whole sort of valorisation of whiteness which goes into this whole thing, even our universities, even our notions of what it means to be human, all of these things ...

'So ... the question for me, what if there were no white people, well I think the thing is that it's sort of an interesting hypothetical question for a mind game but the truth is it's ahistorical and we can't get outside of the history that we inherited and the fact of 500 years of white supremacy ...'

Andile discounts my theory of a new establishment. 'I mean I don't know this world of yours, where you feel South Africa is so black. I mean, really. I mean we're speaking in English now. If you look at television, the people who now get employed are black people who must sound white.'

My colleague, Gugulethu (Gugu) Mhlungu, another key

shaper of the present race debate says, 'Where does the idea that straight long hair is desirable come from? Where does the idea that if you are a certain shade of brown, or if you look a certain way because your nose is a certain way, your lips are a certain thickness, that's beautiful.

'Even ideas of beauty, black beauty, are invariably usually around acceptable forms of blackness, which are often defined by whiteness.'

She continues, 'Even if we were to drive white people into the sea you wouldn't dismantle white supremacy that way.' For her, the new establishment is an imitation. 'The idea of black excellence is black people doing things only white people did previously.'

Establishments are invariably elite. My new establishment is elite – but it is at constant war or in severe discomfort with its elitism, which explains a sub-narrative that needs to understand democratic South Africa as one of white supremacy as it cannot live with the rapid and lively class stratification within black society. It protects bonds of solidarity and Ubuntu by keeping the class contradictions out *there* in the unifying realm offered by theories of white supremacy and whiteness.

Andile is an elite (a former member of parliament, a civil society leader and a senior NGO employee) yet hear him out: 'Black people are servants, workers, the under-class, and that makes us a powerless majority. Black people are a powerless majority and it is a system managed, of course, by other black people. The ANC manages power in the interest of whiteness.

'This is a very common position across South Africa's new

establishment. Until all black people are liberated from poverty, unemployment and inequality then no black people are free, with the implication that whites are to blame.'

I found this conversation with Andile illustrative:

Ferial: So you are saying until more (or all) of our fellow
citizens are not in my position, the system is not working?
Andile: Absolutely.
Ferial: So I can't say, hey, when I look at you, you control the
narrative?
Andile: I wish I did.

And this one with Andile's friend Ziyana Lategan:

Ferial: You look like someone who could make any choice in the
world?
Ziyana: I don't know. Could I?

And this one with Gugu:

Verashni Pillay tells Gugu: I feel like your capital is stronger
than white people's capital in City Press.
Gugu: You need to understand that City Press, *its nature is anti*
the hegemony ...
[Then, I ask a question.]
Ferial: Do you feel acted on?
Gugu: Absolutely. All the time even when you're at the
pinnacle ...

And Gugu is at the pinnacle, in my opinion. She is a cultural pacesetter, in demand here and abroad for her pithy observations and fluid writing style as well as for her social media smarts.

I push my fellow discussants. 'Why don't you change it? You occupy positions of authority …'

Gugu says: 'But if the idea of black excellence is Beyoncé, Bonang [Matheba], Sizwe Dhlomo … you create a new kind of hegemony. For instance, the idea of black excellence in this country is actually premised on the elite, the minority, the people who somehow through some great change managed to transcend everything else and be exceptional. And even that, the idea of framing a whole culture or a standard on an elite is, you know, you don't fix it that way.'

———

When I arrived at *City Press* in 2009, I loved a lot about the place. It has a caring atmosphere that calmed my jagged edges. Our people have a lovely sense of humour and the newsroom is unendingly welcoming, whether it is to a Sudanese delegation of journalists or to MPs straight from the Burkinabé revolution or to visiting foreign interns who have often made a home in our walls for weeks or months at a time.

But the one aspect that perplexed me was the sense of being powerless.

The microwave did not work, highly inconveniencing journalists who tend to eat at their desks or in the tearoom. The fridge broke down and made things more uncomfortable. Promotions were not made. Subscriptions were needed. Whenever we held meetings, there was a section called 'issues' – an innovation meant to deal with workplace issues. As we went through the microwave issue for the umpteenth time, I asked who was responsible. It was 'they'.

For months, I prodded about the 'they' and it was an amorphous power up there, somewhere. In fact, *City Press* is responsible for its own budget and once we'd worked out the system, we could buy microwaves, fridges, tablets and phones within existing procurement systems and budgets.

It gave me a first-hand insight into how power and disempowerment work and how agency is perceived or not perceived even when people's titles gave them authority. When I had worked in majority-white newsrooms, there was no such hesitation as even young white editors presumed an authority to use their power and agency.

At the South African Broadcasting Corporation (SABC), where I spent several years in radio and television from 1993, the apartheid distribution of power centres was self-evident. White journalists got all the new equipment and us black people got the hand-me-downs; bullying by Broederbond editors was common.

A generation of journalists who came to work at the SABC after 1994 did not sit down in the face of this. We objected and organised, demanded and insisted. The courage and the ability to do this flowed straight from growing up in an era of high civic, student and workplace mobilisation. This culture of organising and being able to engage power is not as commonplace as it was – it has left a gap, which has been filled by the whiteness and white supremacy that is, at once, deeply empowering and disturbingly disempowering.

It is empowering because it forms the umbrella study that resonates with a generation of South Africans born free but in chains. It is disempowering because I've seen how it can make a wonderful generation of people see remnant white power as bigger than it really is.

Because social justice is a work in progress, the state is regarded as supremacist. Says Andile: 'Black people can be shot and killed and there is no one that can be held responsible [he is speaking about Marikana] … Andries Tatane shot by the state for demanding water. [Tatane was a Free State activist killed by police while on a protest march. His killing was filmed.]'

I ask: 'But he wasn't shot by white people?'

Researcher and journalist Verashni Pillay asks: 'It's interesting that you're talking about white people and [bald] politicians in the same sense there.'

To which Andile replies: 'Yes, of course, I would.'

For Gugu, it is more bald. She is a scholar of inter-sectionality, the idea that all oppressions (sexual, sexuality, gender, economic) are related and that the transition to democracy ushered in a neoliberal establishment. Neoliberal, in this context, refers to a conservative economic policy that influenced the new political establishment in 1994 to make only small cosmetic changes and not to overthrow the edifice.

She avers: 'You can argue that the ANC government is almost a white supremacist government because we're neoliberal and *that* in this country is hugely anti-black. We've kind of left patriarchy untouched, which for me is also anti-black. Because black women are the majority in this country, if you leave a system like patriarchy, you're leaving a system to screw over the majority.

'I think [black political power] is important but it's not enough. Political power, yes it is important, but that's all it is. It doesn't necessarily translate to other kinds of power.'

———

At first, when I come across whiteness studies, impatience wells in me. It feels like whites are again at the centre of the gaze of the academies. I attend a conference on the topic (and can't believe there's a conference on the topic) where there are almost no black people present. Research is presented and all I hear is white anxiety about its privilege.

It is my first encounter with the field and a researcher presents focus-group studies. In one vignette that stays with me, a respondent angsts about the fact that her family had a swimming pool growing up. This sums it up for me and I am all harrumph with impatience. Who cares, lady?

So, at first, I close my ears and mock the field.

But later, I hear the terms *whiteness* and *white supremacy* everywhere and dominantly in the discourse of a new generation of influencers, such as Milisuthando Bongela, Osiame Molefe and Gugu Mhlungu, among others.

Impatience wells some more. But here, my explanation trips

even me up. What was I feeling? Was it a discomfort that my rainbow nation had frayed edges? Was I empathising with white colleagues and friends? I reflected deeply on this – what in it discomforted me so and continues to discomfort me?

It is a field of study that resonates deeply with an entire generation of young black influencers who want whites to acknowledge their privilege.

Later, I sit in on one of the dozens of sessions I've attended on media transformation. There, my colleague Stephen Grootes of Eyewitness News says sorry for something and the hall of largely ANC-supporting communicators erupts in applause. South Africa wants the moment of national contrition from white South Africa that our founding father Nelson Mandela did not insist upon when power changed hands. The research I grew so deeply despondent about at the whiteness seminar is precisely what black South Africans need to hear – an acknowledgement of white privilege and its distorting effect on black lives voiced by white people. Acknowledgement is a first step towards action.

I want South Africa to be like Vietnam and China, which have shrugged off painful history to claim places as global growth leaders. I want to look back at this South Africa one day and feel as awestruck as I did when I looked at old pictures of Singapore when it was a small and poverty-stricken port and see how it has grown to be a hub of the South East Asian economies.

Economic growth, especially when it is state-supported or developmental, has phenomenal domino effects on generations. Tens of millions of people get lifted from poverty – if greater numbers of people are in work, then the fiscus can more substantially help those left behind. I want the generation that defines my world to take us forward; to be unambiguously ambitious about owning the future because I think they own the present. Turns out I am hopelessly out of touch.

The shade that the whiteness and white supremacy narrative takes in South Africa is inevitably backward focused. It is an anger and a reckoning with the past by a generation that is free (and born free) and completely unenamoured with my generation's rainbow nation naivety and nostalgia. It is the unfinished business of apartheid being taken up by a generation free of the uhuru gratitude that I reflect.

As we hurtled forward in the early 1990s, making our Constitution and then making this nation, psychologists and sociologists and activists such as Pumla Gobodo-Madikizela, Terry Bell and Dumisa Ntsebeza warned against the unfinished business. That business is catching up. Loudly. Scarily. Persistently. In my newsroom at *City Press*, colleagues call it the second revolution. Its shock troops are young. Black. Bright. Powerful. Everywhere. And enraged.

Melissa feels whiteness to be immutable and omnipresent. 'But what I do want to say is that we do know it is shifting. We know that it is globally dominating but we also do know that it is shifting because we wouldn't be able to name it if it weren't. For a very, very long time, people couldn't name it, we didn't have a concept of whiteness, we couldn't talk about this thing and when we first started working in this field we all said well what is it that we're talking about, what is it that we're naming because we're struggling to articulate what it was that we were trying to name as a power relationship.

'So I think we've made great strides in that way. And the fact that it's become so visible, I think that we're seeing an absolute explosion in South Africa of writing, of everybody who is getting a handle on this concept [of whiteness], which we didn't have before.

'This to me is a very, very positive thing because it means it's being grappled with. What will emerge, we don't know. We don't know what the blackness will be that will emerge on the other side – what our sense of the human will be that will emerge on the other side of this. But it is very important that it is being named and that we've got a bit of a handle on it.'

It's everywhere, that's for sure. Often when I listen in on conversations in the *City Press* newsroom, people are talking about white privilege and whiteness in tones that imply at once disgust and confidence to name and shame it. It is on radio, on television. It jumps out of the liberal academies and onto the opinion pages and from those onto radio and television. It is a wave. I feel drowned but also compelled to find out more – I am interested now as my impatience wanes.

This book's title is born from my own style, which is to seek solutions and move on. I guess this is because of my vocation. In our world of relentless deadlines, you find solutions to fill holes quickly and move on to the next thing. And so I think the question is, *Well, what if there were no whites?*

Melissa comments, 'It's a whole new cultural, intellectual process of subjectification, subject formation. I think these are travelling, these are moving, these are in process. I don't think we know what it's going to be but I don't think there's a way of going abracadabra "let's have whiteness disappear".'

For Andile, 'It's a silly question, a silly title that's just going to make sure it trivialises the whole race problem. Okay, if there were no white people … [but] they're here and they fucked us up, bra. That is the fact; that is the reality. [He pounds the table.]'

For Gugu, my question is 'a distraction'. I prod her. 'Gugu, when I see you, I think whatever she wants, the world is ready to give to her. And if there were no whites, then perhaps you would be able to see that.'

To which she replies, 'Oh God, there'd still be men. And capitalism. Part of the imagining of a utopia is also being willing to destroy yourself. So if you were to seriously commit to a thing that was like that, it would entail destroying things that make us as well … that thing that benefits you.

'And a lot of the time, if you look at the way in which we have done revolutions, transferences of power, very few groups have committed to that. I mean the ANC didn't commit to the thing that would unmake them. They were like "we're going to tinker with this" but they really kept the things that make them.

'[This resulted in] a narrative that wiped the slate clean. [White people can say] "No, I'm not racist, I have black friends, no, it's not racism." Having to explain when people say to you

"You speak so well" – that it's racist to say so. It's seen as a com-
pliment. You speak so well. You are so articulate. That comes
from a place that says I am exceptional. And part of the narrative
around our democracy [of a rainbow nation and a miracle] has
made it so hard to then try to explain how things are still a bit
shitty … if you're a woman, if you're black, if you're poor.'

———

The three people at my first learning round table say that the
structures of the past remain unchanged and that the discourse
has allowed the problems to be reframed as black corruption,
black criminality, black incompetence and what Andile calls
'Black Nkandla'.

We are what we are – a diverse country battling the legacy of
apartheid and colonialism. Like Singapore is divided into distinct
ethnic groups, South Africa is divided into four racial groups.
Whites. Africans. Indians. Coloureds. My question *What if there
were no whites* is to think what our future might look like when
the idea of whites still holding such overwhelming power is
loosened.

Most people I speak to can't or won't go there as if it is too
hard to imagine. But it is an exploration that must be made or
the discourse can become dispiriting and distracting. The people
who shaped the Constitution and the transfer of power had
much more reason than our generation to remain mired in white
supremacy then. It was omniscient and not mediated by the

Constitution and a series of laws meant to claw the present loose from the past. It did not have the leverage that freedom gives and that generation was not disabled by it.

These laws include workplace laws; economic policy laws on empowerment; an encyclopedia of land policies and regulations to undo the ravages of the 1913 Land Act; a system of education that has several times been reworked to rewrite Bantu Education. This provides a context to reshape power.

Andile comments: 'Aime Cesaire says we must start from the beginning and demand one thing and that is the end of the world … When I talk to my black radical friends we understand what that means: that approximating freedom for us would mean what Cesaire said. But in the liberal rational world that makes black demands impossible; one cannot entertain meditating about this possibility. We have to be polite and talk about rights and the Constitution and Nelson Mandela.'

For Melissa: 'The question *What if there were no whites* can't be asked because the power of whiteness, its deep construction, has constructed the world that we've got in many, many kinds of ways.'

———

We hold this first round table of my quest for understanding as the #RhodesMustFall movement sets South Africa alight. The #RhodesMustFall movement used the colonial-era statue of Cecil John Rhodes to focus on the incomplete journey of transformation at the University of Cape Town. As the numbers of black students grew over the years at UCT, so did the issues they faced, including cultural alienation, study costs, the dominant culture of the campus, the plight of black academics (and their paltry representation).

The monument becomes the beachhead that contains all the grievances, and students demand #RhodesMustFall. The ANC's policy on apartheid's physical legacy and heritage was interesting. The party decided that the heritage of the past would live in the present (statues, buildings, monuments) as a reminder of the past so it would not be repeated but also as a symbol of strength.

Keeping them in place was not to valorise or honour what Rhodes or Louis Botha or Jan van Riebeeck symbolised, but as a sign of confidence. In 2015, that decision was reinterpreted as weakness and as evidence that the first transition had been one of compradors and collaboration with an evil past.

It had yielded to a transition and a Constitution that contained way too many compromises to make sense to a generation of students who threw poo at the statue as a symbol of their rejection of the entire transition from apartheid to democracy.

It was a turning point where the language of compromise and détente that had formed the basis of what many regarded as South Africa's miracle transition was now being pooh-poohed by a generation who had been born free and into what we thought was a country of opportunity.

This is a generational shift, and a seismic one at that, in how South Africa's transition is understood. It's interesting to me that while Frank Chikane – liberation theologian, politician and dem-ocratic South Africa's second director general of the Presidency – is a father of democracy, it is his son, Kgotsi Chikane, who is leading the #RhodesMustFall movement, a second transition.

Andile's words: 'It was always about preserving white civilisa-tion, ultimately. Because if this liberation movement was devoid of white anxiety (or anxiety about whites), it would have spoken in a different language.'

So, as I pursue my quest of understanding why I feel almost completely out of step with a generation I venerate, I realise that what we are living through is a generational shift. Those of us who admire South Africa's transition and have studied the masterclass in pragmatism that underlined the painstaking nego-tiations for freedom are regarded as outmoded by a young, new establishment. We are regarded as compradors for striving for diversity and non-racialism. Non-racialism is, to all intents and purposes, dead.

And there is an additional trend I learn upon reflection.

My experience of freedom has completely shaped my political views and respect of the transition and the new system of laws and opportunities that fundamentally moulded me. I am meant to write my own story in a separate book but I am completely stuck because writing about my childhood stunts me every time I start.

The feeling that hijacks me each time is of having terrible migraines from walking too far every day to get to school and too far to get to madressa (Islamic school). Writing about that time reawakens that pain and I can't or won't. I've shaken the

49

migraines now, but I feel blinded still by the memory of them and by the weight of a too-heavy school bag on my back. As I wrote this, it clicked why absent-minded me will leave the house without most important things, but never without my sunglasses – I have a fear of sun in my eyes branded there by those migraines that taunt me still in my dreams.

I don't know how to describe feeling want and need and deprivation and how to write now, without hurting people I love and of hurting me, of the unprocessed pain of being lumbered with concerns too big for a child. I don't know how to write about muddled child feelings when you knew you shouldn't trouble your stressed mother and penniless father, but your shoes now have holes in them and they really can't make that long, long walk.

I don't know how to write, at any length, about the impact of Bantu Education on me – that I feel shame, still, because I don't know algebra or geometry; that I don't know the great philosophers and philosophies as well as I should despite half a lifetime of reading because these concepts are best threaded into developing brains while at school.

And I am dead scared writing *this* book because I do not believe I have the analytical fluidity that will make it pass muster by the professoriat. And the reason I do not have that is because I was impaled by Bantu Education and then by an insipid experience at Wits, which I abhorred. I only grew into what I could be when I started at the *Mail & Guardian*, so I find it very difficult to write about what I was.

But I have written words galore and made scores of speeches

on the impact of freedom on my life. If it had not been for freedom, I would be living a nightmare that I dreamt too often before the glimmer of change appeared on my horizon. From the time I turned 13, I went out to look for work after school and at weekends because I couldn't ask my parents for the things teenagers need. With a friend, we beat the streets and found part-time work in Joburg central, at Woolworths and Scotts and other spots.

I hated it so much. The tedium of passing hours, of being subservient and being paid a pittance – I dreamt at night that this was to be my life and bit my lip (as I still do now at the thought) and prayed that it shouldn't be. And it so easily could have been.

When I was even younger, I would go to work with my dad at a clothing factory in lower Doornfontein. It made panties, really cool tracksuits and onesies, and I would count them and pack them and earn something from his generous Jewish boss. It could so easily have been my life if freedom had not arrived.

So I thank the leaders, the guerrillas, the activists who gave us freedom, and the ANC, too, for it completely deepened and lengthened my horizons and opened up unimaginable vistas from the times I spent at Georgie-Porgie (the clothing factory) and Woolworths in Hillbrow, asking people their bra sizes or lining up matronly clothes by size. 32. 34. 36. 38. 40.

Freedom has allowed my self-actualisation – to put it in the pop ways of the talks I do: without it, I would not have this dream job. With some 25 ycars of being a journalist, I still marvel every day at the sheer joy of earning my living by doing something I love: stepping into different worlds and then communicating those to readers.

I can support my mom (my dad died a decade ago and left an insurance policy of R10 000.00, no medical aid and no pension). I have a tiny house and a 2004 black Jeep, but mostly, I have well-being, a situation that evaded me for all of my growing-up years. You only know the fundaments of security when you don't have it. And I can pay it forward. So, I feel free and I feel like freedom worked for me. I understand it personally and this has influenced my world view and my politics. I am my politics and my understanding of freedom.

For the generation whose thoughts I am seeking to under-stand, it is different. Gugulethu Mhlungu looks to all intents and purposes like a person with absolute agency, with wide vistas of opportunity and options laid out before her like a buffet of freedom's goodies, but this is my view and one with which she has serious differences.

'For me, it was a combination of chances, like one of the reasons I could go to the school I did was that my gran was a domestic worker for a man who lived in Rosebank so I could go to the school down the road.

'And one of the reasons I could do sort of decently was the man was nice enough to let us use his Internet. The fact that your gran has a decent employer is a massive privilege given what the stakes are.

'And this is the thing [with] the black middle-income class (we're not a real middle class); we're struggling with this kind of privilege, it's not institutionalised, it's not generational but we certainly have a kind of privilege that poor South Africans don't have.'

Andile comments: 'It's absolutely dangerous for black people to generalise their experiences. For instance, Ferial feels that she has overcome all these things. I'm sure I live better than my brothers and the people I come from. I would say maybe 95% of my schoolmates from the farm end up either on the farm as farmworkers or in the township, or they're just fucked. When I talk to them, we come from different worlds. I've forgotten everything about my upbringing with them because so much life has happened for me, right? I can't now say we had equal choices; we didn't.

'Even under apartheid there were some great black men and women, who were successful as business people, who were successful as academics and so on. If you extend your reasoning, you could say: but apartheid is not so bad. Look at those guys, they're doing so well.'

For me the political is intensely personal – freedom has been good for me and to me. I know it's not the same for many, many South Africans, but there are enough of us who have benefited from freedom to build on it. Yet, the generation that so interests me for its absolute rejection of black empowerment and its insistence that we live in a time of white supremacy do not see themselves as an embodiment of the defeat of whiteness and white supremacy.

One day, there is a vision in our newsroom. She has wild, frizzy hair and presence. I can feel the entire newsroom stop as she walks in and I watch as all eyes look over and wonder, Who's that? She feels to all intents and purposes as if she belongs in *City Press* and the cool people seem to know her.

That is Danielle Bowler. Scholar. Artist. Singer. Tweeter. She electrifies spaces. I look at Danielle Bowler and wonder, could I have been a little, just a little, like her if I hadn't grown up when I did. For one: the hair. My hair was impossibly wild growing up and I hated it. Born a hybrid person, hyphenated by apartheid's mad identity brokers, I was called 'Indian/Cape Malay' and lived in two worlds.

I grew up in Bosmont, a coloured area where the West turns wild about 15 minutes in that direction out of Johannesburg. Parts of my family lived in Lenasia or in Fordsburg and in Azaadville. It was a bifurcated life lived across identities and the texture of its different hair strands. I realised my hair was a problem early on. Called upon to be a bridesmaid at about age five, the aunties decided on a hairstyle where you bind little girls' hair in bits of white material and the next morning you have locks.

Not mine. Sorry. The aunty from the Indian part of my family was beside herself. What to do with this child whose hair was standing in wild clumps? I was in tears. I think my silky-maned mother was, too, not quite knowing what to do with an approaching wedding and a daughter who was going to be the embarrassment of the retinue. When I was about eleven years old, I thought, bugger this, and wore an Afro. For about a week. Then the principal's daughter asked me: 'My father asks why your hair is so ugly now?'

I learnt not to like my wild hair and I've spent years torturing it to manageability. It's messed now.

So, Danielle Bowler with her beautiful wild locks that curve and spring and spiral is freedom personified for me. Beyond that, she possesses a confidence that I would have killed for in my twenties and her languid occupation of time and space I find deeply admirable. One of the great sadnesses of my university life is that I spent it in such invisibility, so completely debilitated by the culture of Wits and by the superior confidence of my mostly white fellow students.

Danielle is a scholar of race and identity and part of my second round-table discussion as I explore a race debate I do not fully understand.

I put it to her that I find the omnipresence of the whiteness narrative disempowering, like a hurdle that can't be crossed.

'It can often seem that we're talking about whiteness all the time when we're talking about a linked system [where all oppressions are linked]. These things are confronting and they confront you every day if you let it,' she says.

Her hair and how it is styled gives Danielle access to different worlds. 'If I have straight hair, I can often be read as white and then I will be privy to conversations that people would not normally discuss.'

Like what?

She describes sitting on a bus with a man moaning about black people not knowing what to do with the country as she is stuck next to him for the next few hours. She struggles with the idea of being 'neither here nor there', as she puts it. Tears well up in her eyes.

'I've been having an existential [crisis] lately. I took refuge in blackness and there's now a huge backlash against that kind of Biko blackness ... For me, it's quite a personal hurtful [experience] ... Again, where do you belong?' Biko blackness includes coloureds and Indians as black.

Danielle describes a personal experience of how white privilege can punch you in the stomach and wind you.

'I remember the one day one of my best friends had a 21st birthday party. I walked into her house and I was immediately unseated by anger. I didn't know what was going on [with me]. I felt ill.

'I went to the bathroom, and realised the wealth I was seeing made me so mad. Work has been done [by government], but when you have been affected by things and the state doesn't recognise that, there's lots of anger.'

Multiply this experience by, say, three million (a conservative estimate of black young people in the workplace and at formerly white universities) and you can see the domino effect of learning first-hand how much you don't have and how much privileged people take for granted, which has generated a rage that will not be calmed and is under-tracked in our country.

While marketers worship at the altar of a black middle class, almost every person I spoke to for this book questions the concept because their lives are so different and their responsibilities so much deeper and more profound than the white colleagues and friends they make at universities or at work or socially.

This generation is a beneficiary of affirmative action. Private schools offer scholarships to talented black students because corporates need to satisfy employment equity laws and know they have to feed the pipeline. Two private schools offered Danielle partial scholarships because she was top of her class and with obvious potential.

'I landed up going to a public school and was better off for it … and I got a half scholarship to go to Rhodes [University]. It was fine, except …' She would go home at vacation time and notice 'less stuff in the cupboards, and you feel all that pressure because all their hopes are on you'. That's a lot of pressure. 'At university you're on a scholarship, [and] your scholarship can't cover everything. For months you're living off baked beans, you walk outside and everything looks right but you're in tears at home.'

Even today, with a few degrees under her belt, it's still tough. Danielle can't afford a car and doesn't want the balloon payment that is often the only way of owning one.

She says: 'Where you're at is this halfway station to freedom. It's that strange experience. Just feeling that kind of burden of social mobility and trying to entrench yourself in the middle class [is hard]. Because of capitalism and patriarchy and the way they entrench themselves, it's a hurdle to getting yourself safely there.'

For a generation of young black professionals and workers, success in corporate South Africa seems to mean that you need to check your blackness in at the door, to divest yourself of your identity to succeed in a culture that is still overwhelmingly white in demographics and therefore in culture if current employment equity statistics are a barometer.

For liberal, rainbow nation me, this is a whole education and, in at least two examples, I am guilty. 'Why don't you look at me?' I remember nagging a reporter when he worked at the *Mail & Guardian* when I was political editor. It felt odd to have somebody looking down as they spoke, but, as he explained, in isiXhosa culture, you don't look an elder in the eye.

My second realisation is bigger and more formative for me. In my insistence on creating rainbow nation workplaces, what have I suppressed?

Danielle says: 'When you enter white spaces, [there is] pressure to leave your blackness at the door. Everything that has to do with whiteness has value, [you must] put your blackness in a box to go about your work.'

Like how?

Language. Culture. Values. English is not regarded as a lingua franca but as a fundament of whiteness. Workplace cultures are designed around Anglo-Saxon dominant culture (the firm handshake, the eye contact, the networks, the practices and 'codes' that are acceptable). Accents.

Danielle recalls her accent changing between her white school and her coloured home. Her teachers told her to burnish her white accent and to retain it when she tried to push back against how she was being made to sound.

A certain accent can affect how people are treated and perceived. It seems that when individuals live their identities or do not know the codes of working life, it is possible to hear negative perceptions of them – 'I don't want that person on my team; they don't have enough confidence', is the type of comment reported.

The opportunities available as a result of the pressures of black empowerment might have led to bursaries and opportunities for some young people, but at the same time the pressures to fit into a middle-class life can come at the expense of a sense of social justice; a disconnect in terms of benefiting from a system that is still based on the existence of an under-class.

I ask those at the round table what their good society would look like.

Now loving the Mapungubwe Institute for Strategic Reflection (MISTRA) where she works, Danielle has found what transformation may look like and be experienced as. 'Often when I have to go to an interview, if not in arts or media, my Afro is going to denote something: that I'm political, that I have no decorum or polish. Blackness denotes a negativity.

'MISTRA is such a black space, it's overwhelming. I went into a canteen and someone was eating a sheep's head [*skop* – from the Afrikaans colloquial *skaapkop*].

'This is what a transformed society would look like. We don't want just big things, like access to jobs, economic power. We want the ability to speak in our accents ... things that white people take for granted because white people move around the world with ease.

'bell hooks [the black American poet, feminist and social activist] says oppression is the absence of choice ... [It would be] a world where people have more choices.'

———

My experience and knowledge is of white South Africans as a minority group getting smaller in numbers and power and fitting into the new South Africa but no longer running it. But if you listen to our country's race debate, it is as if there is an equal number of black and white people in South Africa or as if blacks are an oppressed minority and whites a majority.

In all the interviews, I test this theory and ask how many whites there are in South Africa. The answers range from wrong (estimates that are high but not as high as my thesis would suggest) to impatient in that it is held to be a stupid question.

It doesn't count, says Danielle, 'Blackness is invisible. You would call this place [Rosebank in Johannesburg] white but we're surrounded by black waiters.'

There is a discussion around the fact that whiteness extends beyond people; it's as much a system as a group of individuals.

Danielle adds: 'If we took them [white people] out right now, we would continue white supremacy.'

———

For the umpteenth time in my journey through this book, I feel defeated by my uhuru generation. If whiteness and white supremacy are held to be so immutable and intrinsic, then they are unbeatable. I guess I grew up in a time of greater hope and faith in black power, when liberation movements that had little beyond people power and global solidarity would brook no such thoughts about apartheid and the stranglehold it had on us. From school to the early years of working life, our life was one measured by 'when apartheid ends ...' – there was always an end game in sight.

What strikes me with our young power generation is that it

can see no end to white supremacy. My impatience is to see what they are going to do with power and how we are all going to look and be when they get there. Danielle and others comment it is a problem to push people to say what change they want when they ask for it. This revolution will not be hurried along and South African race and identity talk is a work in long progress no matter how impatient a generation like mine gets with it.

And I realise that where I am is caught in a massive generational difference and completely disparate ways of seeing. In addition to my Ray-Bans, I wear rose-coloured spectacles, that's for sure. Take Rosebank, which Danielle and others say is white. I've worked and played there for years and I see it completely differently.

From being a place fed by old white money, it is the party ground of new money and a space where at least a hundred thousand black economic empowerment (BEE) deals have been hatched in the 21 years I've covered the process of empowerment. The waiters are black, but so are most of the patrons and consumers who have made it such a run-away success. My bank account has been held at First National Bank in Rosebank since the Braamfontein branch opposite Wits closed down and became a Ron Hubbard stronghold about 20 years ago, and I've watched the Rosebank branch change from being almost all-white in staff and customers to being almost all-black in staff and customers.

I learn from the round tables that one generation – mine, perhaps – believes hegemony has shifted. This means that there is a new group of influencers who exert authority over society with a distinct set of ideas. I see it everywhere from literature to politics to property.

But the younger generation doesn't believe this shift has yet occurred. Asked if she doesn't think that her and her peers are not creating a new hegemony or at least a counter-hegemony, Danielle says: 'I don't give myself that much credit. I think the narrative [of race and identity; of whiteness and white suprem- acy] is catching fire. But I don't think it's becoming a hegemony. I think we're just getting into newspapers.'

If you read media theorist Noam Chomsky, that is precisely where hegemonic thought is crafted.

'I'm just so fascinated by the idea of the anti-oppressive voice as the new hegemony. That becomes oppressive [itself],' says Danielle. 'I honestly think you give us more credit than we deserve. Incremental change is important. I constantly see ways that I affirm other black people but I don't think that is making as significant a change as you ascribe to it.'

Not for the first time do I discern that power is a difficult cloak to wear comfortably. It is almost easier to default into the language of powerlessness rather than to use your influence and authority to reshape the society the millennials have inherited – and which many clearly do not like.

That the counter-narrative is becoming the dominant narra- tive is pretty clear, though, and it is being aided by social media. The flattening out of communications through platforms such as Facebook and Twitter and the rapid uptake of mobile telephones have enlivened and empowered millions of black young South Africans who have that essential thing: voice, and voice *is* power.

There are examples almost every day of how mobile phones and social platforms are combining to inform a new race and identity activism and to mobilise people.

As the statue of Cecil John Rhodes was removed from its plinth earlier this year, the story was told as #RhodesMustFall – a symbol of how a movement started on social media, then moved into the real world and eventually became so powerful and loud that the statue fell. This happened even though venerated UCT alumni such as struggle veterans George Bizos and Albie Sachs argued for its alteration and retention as an act of memory against forgetting.

3

A WAR WITH YESTERDAY

'Thank you,' an advertising representative says to me, as we settle down into another session of a media conference at which 200 of our industry's leading lights are gathered.

'For what?' I ask.

'For representing.'

Earlier, a headline speaker had said a, frankly, ridiculous thing. Ahistorical too. And provocative. I was, it seemed, the only person provoked by the view that apartheid had been slightly more than 'a little domestic squabble', as the revered speaker had declared it. So I had disagreed and pointed out that apartheid's hard inter-generational impacts were still very present – and that the United Nations had declared the oppressive system a crime against humanity.

There was a frisson in the air as I sat down, but nothing you don't experience as a journalist if you ask an uncomfortable question, so I barely noticed it.

Then an agitated Magazine Maven rose. 'Moving on,' she declared, notably irritated by politics with a capital P. I never understand people who are not interested in how things work, but, hey ... She asked something akin to what the speaker had had for breakfast and everybody breathed a sigh of relief and seemed genuinely more interested in his eating (or reading) habits than in a discussion on our past and present. We moved on.

———

He is a delightful man, given to provocations that come, perhaps, from finely tuned beliefs. In the greater swathe of world history, of course 50-odd years of formal apartheid is a blip. The speaker remarked upon the emerging market giants of India and China where he had seen a generation forging ahead and taking their country with them, reaching for tomorrow. At home he sees South Africans engaged in a battle with yesterday.

The speaker points out (aptly in my view) that young Chinese are not waging war against the Cultural Revolution. Young Indians do not hold a grudge against the Moguls. Instead, they are thrusting ahead.

I had found the same on countless trips to India and one to Vietnam. In Vietnam I had expected to find a people as interested as I was in the war with the United States. Instead, all I found were guides with a dodgy knowledge for whom trips to the museum in Saigon and the Cu Chi Tunnels (in which the Vietcong guerrillas had created underground worlds and so held off superior American firepower) were opportunities only to make money off people like me, who came armed with revolutionary nostalgia and hard currency. To stand terrified and transfixed at a traffic light in Hyderabad or Hanoi, as I have done, was to see the furious pace of growth of India and Vietnam, spurred largely by highly ambitious young people. I was transfixed not by the speed, but by the fear of the speed. If you're not fast there, you can be road kill.

In South Africa, that same younger generation is engaged in a war with yesterday fought on the platforms of tomorrow such as Twitter and Facebook. Even when they have reached the pinnacle of success (or are en route to it), I have detected among this generation a determination to engage a race war and a generation who feel disempowered by life, and mostly by working life. Empowerment comes in the form of social media discussions and what feels to be the liberating philosophical study of whiteness, which has come to trump schools of non-racialism and racial unity as the defining school of thought of our time.

Through that day and the next, I am surprised by the number of my black (and some white) colleagues who tell me variations of well done for speaking up.

My brow furrows now as it did then as I ponder: why didn't you say anything? I find a lot of this around – people will seethe but not speak up. An eighties person like me does not get this. I guess it comes from growing up in a time when you could unionise and when power was something to be engaged.

I guess it is the time I learnt my politics, too, that makes me scratch my head at the aimless fury of the race debate, but the speaker and I come at it from very different places. The fiercely political eighties were very future-directed: this shit had a sell-by date and young people were defining that date more and more closely. I don't believe that apartheid was a short domestic dispute and I believe fervently that you shape your own destiny.

I wonder why my colleagues who encouraged my representing had allowed the Magazine Maven to move on the room so quickly when clearly they had more to say. The moment crystallises a truth for me. Our country is stuck between people who want to move on – for whom the past is a hindrance; and people who feel we can't move on because the past is still their present.

Black people take to Twitter and to the relative echo chamber of Facebook to voice a thousand frustrations and uncertainties that can be characterised as: we just got here, and you want to move on? Already? No ways. There is a cottage industry of blacks-only campaigns, whiteness conferences and columns of painful accounts of remnant white privilege that define the time.

It informs the title of this book. What if there were no whites? I feel it is the subtext of the time: if there were no whites, then everything would be okay. Except it wouldn't. The movement has become a palliative, a fix-it for the burdens of the black middle class squashed by impossible demands; it has also become the smokescreen for a proud liberation movement that has evolved into a so-so government to hang all its failures on. It has become the place for the workplace war that the niceties of corporate life do not allow. This is not to say corporate life is nice. From my early studies of post-apartheid working life, cultures have not shifted at all and remain Western and white.

The geography of the race debate has very little to do with the larger requirements of social justice, but it is, 20-odd years into democracy, the only bellwether of how to judge South African race relations. The crucible.

It's all we have to judge because it's the only place where

black and white South Africans engage each other – the work-place, the suburbs, restaurants, clubs and gyms.

The view? Not great. The rainbow nation? As ephemeral, beautiful and fragile as the phenomenon it is named for.

Many white people genuinely just want to move on – not in the psychologically healthy sense of moving on but in the amnesiac sense. Why must a new generation bear the price and burdens of the old? And they are literally moving on. The rate and pace of white migration from South Africa is a story that is not well told. Whenever I ask groups of people what percentage of the population whites comprise, it is inevitably higher than the real total. The view is the same among blacks and whites and it tells me that whites amplify their power in South Africa and blacks do the same about whites.

The questions (and answers) help me understand a lot of the race debate in South Africa. So, instead of being understood as a declining minority, whites are still perceived to be a powerful majority despite the latest population projections putting whites at 8.4% of the population, down from 10.9% in 1996 in the first democratic census that counted all of us accurately.

My first major encounter with the culture of moving on came in 2012 when Woolworths faced a boycott call for an advertisement for black candidates to fill certain jobs. The campaign it faced was one of the first great instances of social media activism (or racism, depending where you stand) with a drive to boycott Woolworths hosted on Facebook, Twitter and other social platforms.

Very soon, the philosophical and legal underpinnings of the

campaign came to inform a much larger drive in South Africa underwritten by the trade union Solidarity and its civil society arm Afriforum, a white rights protection organisation that rails against employment equity even as report after report reveals that at senior levels of the private economy there are no significant racial shifts.

Yet if you were a Plutonian who fell to earth, you would swear that there was large-scale displacement of whites by blacks in South Africa. It is simply not so.

White top managers continue to dominate, with mahogany row as it always was. In 2003 seven in ten top managers were white. By 2013, the number was six in ten and when I checked in 2015, it was the same.

The actual data of employees in top management is revealing. According to mandatory reports to the employment equity commission, the total number of employees in the top management category showed that of a total of 22 571 top managers recorded, 14 149 were white. This was followed by African managers at a mere 4 464, Indian managers at 1 879 and coloured managers at 1 146.

At senior management, there is faster change. Whites comprise 57% of all senior managers, with broad black groups making up 40% and imported managers the rest. At the professional level (the next most senior), the 2015 figures reveal that equity is in sight. At the professionally qualified level, the total workforce increased to 22 571 individuals in ten years with six in ten of these new professionals being African. This is good progress but something is holding up the catapult into the top suites.

At the skilled level – the next level of measure of workplace progress – the story gets better. In percentage representation terms, the various groups seem to be doing well at the skilled level.

Why do numbers matter? They are the only rational barometer of whether working society is changing. A life of realisable aspiration requires workplaces that reflect the diversity of the country. The numbers are a real-world indicator of whether the twin peaks of apartheid – job reservation and Bantu Education – are being unwound by the march of freedom. But the theory of moving on carries with it a corollary. In my experience, the South African private sector declares itself or thinks itself transformed and ready to move on when there are only slightly more than a handful of black people in positions of significant authority. In fact, to genuinely exist as corporate citizens, as many profess to be, the corporates should more clearly reflect the society they exist in. In my many discussions with a variety of South Africans, it is clear that workplace cultures are still bewildering and isolating for many black South Africans. If the effective measure of corporate power is a number of black people or even an equal number of black people, we will continue to be stuck.

———

The Magazine Maven and the Woolworths Boycott Brigade are my two learning curves of the culture of moving on. At the time of the attempted Woolworths boycott, I penned an article for News24 that generated such trolling it helped me construct the thick skin you need to play in the race space in South Africa.

Back when I scraped into Wits, I marvelled at the new white friends I made. They all had straight teeth and they all had driver's licences and cars. And they knew all the answers in those huge lecture theatres and sometimes, for goodness sake, they even knew the lecturers. Wow. Gifted people, I thought then, not having an understanding or knowledge of white privilege, the intergenerational transfer of well-being and privilege.

When I look back now, it strikes me that all the people I met lacked an understanding of how unusual they were in the greater scheme of things. Their cars. Braces. Privilege. Holidays. Tutors. Networks. This was the bill of rights of being born white. When I look at an issue now, I see that this is still how the world looks for a generation who encounters a glass ceiling.

They shopped at Woolworths. I worked there on Friday afternoons and Saturdays.

In the lecture theatres, even when I knew the answers, I did not answer, a practice I only learnt much later was a form of internalised inferiority – put there by a system that told us repeatedly that we were people of a lesser god. In my school, very few of us made it to university – most left to join the ranks of the destined roles for coloured people.

Then, it was to become a clothing worker (my family largely worked in the rag trade before the industry went to the wall) or at the top end to become a low-level bank clerk or a junior teacher. There is nothing wrong with those roles, but it is wrong when that is your predetermined destiny.

Today, I feature as an alumnus Wits is proud of; in reality, my relationship with that alma mater is far more ambivalent than the campaigns I've featured in suggest. I was a terrible student – ill-prepared for university life by coloured education. Our system, until matric, had been geared towards rote learning and never to self-study, analysis and the Socratic discussion that underpins university life. It was an alien world and, when I look back now, I realise I made absolutely no effort to succeed in it and preferred the radical student activism that gripped the place in the mid-1980s.

Faced with the superior confidence and skills and the domination of discussion by white students, I retreated, convinced I was unable to compete. If there had been social media then, I would sound like a generation now sounds – angry and *gatvol* at the automatic privilege I encountered, a privilege that did not even know its name.

Some of my coloured friends had lovely teeth, but most of us were dentally imperfect with gaps, crowds and overlaps that would make my present dentist weep. And almost none of us could drive. Hell, no. I bused it in belching Putco buses from Bosmont or took a train to Fietas (Pageview) and then walked. My friends from Lens (Lenasia) went home on rattling, windblown buses and most of my black friends took ramshackle buses to Soweto residences.

This made late study hard and getting to campus a little hazardous. Nowadays, I speed along that road from Mayfair through Braamfontein when I come home from my mum's house and I shiver with relief that I made it back safely on this route that I now recognise to have been pretty risky for a young woman to traverse.

Do I write this because I feel sorry for myself? Not at all. All that walking gifted me with good fitness. I tell the story to illustrate privilege and how it is passed on.

The only reason a generation of us were able to clamber out of one class, out of a distorted destiny, was because of employment equity. From university into the world of work, we have required help to get a place at the table not because we are 'stupid' but because of the structural blocking of opportunity. I am deeply grateful for my place at the table; the opportunities it enshrined have enabled me to live my dreams.

Without affirmative action, I would likely be a retrenched clothing factory worker or a low-level banking clerk. That was the expected, the planned outcome for people like me. The system was called apartheid. We needed help to escape our destiny and millions of South Africans still need that help.

It is not reverse racism, but a constitutional imperative to fix our society. Affirmative action is enshrined in our Constitution. Solidarity, Afriforum and those of you who spammed the Woolies CEO for applying the law are wrong. It discounts, completely, the role of intergenerational privilege in your life.

To make a good future society demands we have make-right policies for the old one. It doesn't fix itself.

At several newspapers where I've edited, there is always an issue because young black journalists, in the main, cannot drive when they get into the newsroom. Like I could not. Often, white colleagues complain at being made to chauffeur. We make a plan because some of us know that it was pretty hard to learn to drive if you didn't grow up with a car in your home.

Extrapolate this into South African corporate life and there are other examples, such as doing presentations, building networks, coping with the disciplines of working life, self-confidence. All these are learnt skills that come with middle-class privilege.

Privilege is intergenerational and it includes small things and big things: good teeth, driver's licences, a financial helping hand from parents and social networks, the easy navigation of the halls of power – all of which are forms of capital that are unacknowledged in the toxic ways we speak about employment equity. Twenty-one years after apartheid, we are not yet playing on an even field, especially in corporate and working life in the private sector.

The impacts of privilege are only now being explored in South Africa by black South Africans and the term 'white privilege' has come to be used almost pejoratively by black South Africans at the same time as a new generation of young white South Africans eschews any acknowledgement of it.

My sense of why workplaces have not changed sufficiently is because people are blind to privilege and how their racial filters see talent and potential. Often, in my experience, managers view this in their own image. And so they will progress and bond with people who look and talk like them. It requires no less than an act of political consciousness not to do this because we are all, after all, victims of apartheid in one or other way.

White managers frequently do not see it. Let me provide two examples from an industry I love – the media.

When a new editor took over *Business Times*, the highly regarded business section of the *Sunday Times*, he injected verve and a swashbuckling spirit into it. I often turned to that section first because he made it so attractive and a must-read. But what surprised me was the handful of columnists he chose. Bruce Whitfield. Duncan McLeod. Jeremy Maggs. Ann Crotty. Arthur Goldstuck. After 20-odd years of freedom, he could not find a single black regular columnist to take the weekly business pulse. Of course, each of the columnists he chose is an industry specialist and each is brilliant at what he (and the one she) does, but it is a pattern I see repeatedly in the media.

When I worked at the hallowed *Financial Mail*, one of the first times I learnt how to cause a frisson was when I asked why not one of its seven columnists was black, and that was in 1999. There was agitation and a great shifting of chairs before the editor also decided it was time to move on from that discussion.

Too often, still, I look at a magazine's masthead and am amazed that at this point in our history they can find no black writers or editors. Because it's an industry (or craft) I know and love well, I am also aware that it is the outcome of networks and privileges that have not sufficiently shifted to make us a normal society.

I hear managers saying that in the battle between efficiency and equality, efficiency will win and equality will often mean someone who looks like them and with whom they feel they can accomplish their goals. And in all these ways, the media is an adequate barometer of the society it reports upon.

It is pretty informed experience now that when you have a white editor, then the numbers of white columnists will be high. But black editors will generally run more diverse titles or broadcast programmes that reflect more of South Africa's people. When one editor quit the *Business Times*, his replacement almost immediately had a range of black columnists writing for the publication, including Ziphozakhe Sikhakhane and Jabulani Sikhakhane.

To make South Africa successful, we have to play the long game and employment equity is an essential component of that success. The amazing growth of a black middle class that has kept our economy afloat is the outcome not of BEE but of employment equity. BEE is largely a stalled and elite process while employment equity has delivered national goods. Viewed this way, we have all benefited from the policy, but with a full frontal attack on the policy, the pace is slowing.

I often speak publicly to South African businesses and while there is progress at some, in many industries it's pretty clear who continues to rule the roost. And my experience at *City Press* has been an eye-opener.

The *Mail & Guardian* is, I realise with hindsight, an unusual newsroom. People cohere around a set of journalistic values that go from spunk and cheek to thumbing your nose at authority. It is highly political, with a stance that largely supports the liberation movements and black politics. It has had its transformation moments (I led a few in my time) but on the whole, the paper did not have fracturing race debates. The baton was passed fairly smoothly from Mondli Makhanya to me and then to Nic Dawes.

So, when I am approached to edit *City Press*, I agree as I think it may be interesting to learn something new. My brief is clear. Turn the Pan-Africanist title into one that is comfortable in all homes. In other words, shift its racial demographic and its class profile. I worry vaguely about how Pan Africanists will accept my Steve Biko definition of black, which includes coloured and Indian people but ultimately accept the new role as a great opportunity.

City Press is loving and kind. Its people are endlessly stylish. I start part-time and sound out every person who works there on how they see the title, what their bond to it is and what they would like to see change. As it turns out, the team writes my job description. With few exceptions, they want a move into a different era with new content and a distinct look. That's fine. They aspire to particular and better lives as the South African rising middle class does. We all want better business and arts coverage. All's good. Until it isn't.

City Press is about 98% black but for two or three white colleagues who are black in spirit. It is homogenous in its thought and one-dimensional in its football support. This is a yellow (Chiefs) newsroom and I am a black buccaneer (Pirates). I am non-racialist in the Mandela tradition; this is a Pan-Africanist newsroom. One of my skills is blending political coverage, so this is not a problem; I had been doing it for 20 years as a journalist making sure the entire spectrum of political life is covered. But, then, I employ an assistant editor who can drive a feisty news agenda. He is white and Afrikaans. In turn, he employs a highly talented news editor who is yellow but white. And I choose a white features editor.

All the time, I have my eyes on our racial make-up as I try to move my newsroom to match the country, more or less. I'm not a Verwoerdian racial bean-counter, but I do know the value of diverse newsrooms.

It goes pear-shaped. From the petty to the hegemonic debate, it is trouble. And here I learn. When the rugby is on, the television can be loud. When the soccer is on, there is much shush-shushing going on. There are white turned-up noses at *skop* – the sheep's-head breakfast of the guys on a Saturday morning; the energy to fuel them through our impossibly punishing deadline days. When the Afrikaans assistant editor tries to invite his black editor colleagues to lunch at the Service Station (a hipster joint with insubstantial hipster food in Melville) they leave because there isn't enough meat.

There is obstinacy when the assistant editor tries to introduce rugby into the black and yellow mix. Rugby? What the hell? This is *City Press*.

I bring Max du Preez in as a columnist to *City Press* and he is rejected by staff and readers alike and, in the end, he fires us.

The natural confidence of the new editors is like oil on water to the *City Press* spirit. They are, I don't know how to put it, too self-assured and confident. It is as if they just came in and took over, a colleague tells me. The news editor's style I hired her for (opinionated, sharp-witted, to the point) is read as arrogant and know-it-all to a team that prefers a softer, kinder touch. In my experience, black people speak to each other and others differently with a greater deference and respect.

One of the best writers leaves because he won't be told what to do by two white women – for him, my moves are like a return to *baasskap*, I hear later. To me, his stance is like apartheid redux. You are objecting to colleagues simply because they are white, I tell my newsroom. When I show my colleagues the equity figures we keep updated, it matters not a bit; I have upset the power balance too much. I learn a lesson or three.

It all explodes. We are across every front page in the country. I am chastened. And wiser about how working spaces and media operate. Years later, the black sports editor complains that a white subeditor's notes are sharp and sarcastic (as subeditors often are). I know what to do now but only because I've walked through the fire. *City Press* is a microcosm of South African life and of a trend I come to discern more and more clearly: black people want their own space to be; and they want hegemony in other spaces.

Black majority spaces are, in my experience, more tolerant and considerate; age respect is important and how we speak to each other even more important. It is often at significant odds with the white Western culture of many South African workplaces.

———

What if there were no whites? Many people, in my experience, largely want to be apart rather than together. But it's not a life I want to live. It would feel too much like, well, apartheid. But *City Press* has taught me the cultural nuances and step changes of real change and my politics is terribly out of step. Social media has also taught me how out of step I am. And it has informed me that many black people desire all-black spaces in which to navigate new freedoms and establish new borders and independence.

The race war has moved from where it was fought under apartheid into the ether, the digital life where websites and social media host the painful identity war. Here's an example. It is women's month and events flow thick and fast. One catches my attention. #ForBlackGirlsOnly. The organisers ask for a specialist and I tweet a question about how an event #ForWhiteGirlsOnly would wash among the people I follow and in the social community I find captures a zeitgeist.

People are furious. It teaches me something more. For one: many young women want to be signed up for the event – the concept is American and creates safe circles of solidarity and voice. It turns out that black women I follow on Twitter believe it is still vital for South Africa. My question provokes a rage I had last seen when I wrote the letter to young white people who wanted to boycott Woolworths – the moving-on camp.

This is the other camp. These are largely young South Africans who believe the country has moved nowhere and that blacks-only events are vital to find identity and space in which to be and to grow. I guess things have not moved on from the time I went to Wits and immediately gravitated to the Black Students' Society or the largely black socialist organisations that wanted to smash the system. The responses enlightened me:

- ❏ Sometimes black women just need a place where they can be free from the aggressions they face daily.
- ❏ Asking this [what would happen with a #ForWhiteGirlsOnly event] can be compared to asking why there is no Man's month … it's just irrelevant.

❏ As someone out there already tweeted 'Life is #ForWhiteGirlsOnly'.

❏ Do you not understand why black women would feel the need to have a space to be themselves in South Africa?

❏ #ForWhiteGirlsOnly is a continuation of everyday life.

❏ White lawyers do have a white association. It may not be registered, but it exists …

❏ When it comes to standards of beauty, etc., a white norm is assumed. Black women need to speak for themselves.

❏ That [#ForWhiteGirlsOnly] exists already. It's called mainstream feminism.

❏ #ForWhiteGirlsOnly has been going on for over 300 years.

❏ Black South Africans are oppressed; black South Africans don't enjoy economic or social influence. It still rests in the hands of [the] white South African minority.

❏ Your question's disappointing because you are a black woman. Black South Africans enjoy only political dominance.

❏ It's equivalent to why we need a Black Lawyers Association.

❏ Why do black people have to accommodate and centre white people when it comes to our issues? We aren't here to coddle whiteness.

❏ But you should know the answer to this question, sis. You live in SA. You understand our experiences. Don't you?

❏ [#WhiteGirlsOnly events would be] an unnecessary perpetuation of an already existing sense of entitlement.

❏ #WhiteGirlsOnly events would be what the world is already.

❏ #WhiteGirlsOnly events would [make us] think white

women are whiting and trying to colonise the spaces of marginalised people as usual.

❑ White women have plenty of safe spaces to engage and just be. Why take issue with black women creating such spaces.

❑ The question [what would you think of a #WhiteGirlsOnly event] centres white girls. Centring black girls is important.

The idea of centring interests me – young black people want to occupy the centre; to nudge white young people from a centre they still believe does not belong to them.

It is a theme I come across almost weekly of people feeling marginalised.

But in too much that I read and observe, the concept is not to occupy on equal terms – what is needed or desired is a sort of new dominion or *baasskap* to replace an old one, a new ruling class instead of a new establishment.

The other is a notion I come across again and again and again – the idea that black people have only won political *freedom* and that political *power* is only in office, but not in power. My research is replete with black people feeling marginalised – a majority still marginalised by a minority, as if apartheid has only been nudged off-centre but that, to all intents and purposes, it continues to exist. The third notion I learn is the view that empowerment happens in blacks-only settings such as the #ForBlackGirlsOnly meetings in women's month.

In my opinion, the finest interpreter of our maladies is Milisuthando Bongela who runs a feminist stokvel to reflect upon what it means to be young, black and conscious right here right now. A Rhodes alumnus, she found her white friends planned different lives after graduation than she did. 'When I went home to tell my parents that I, like my white friends, was considering working on a kibbutz in Israel for a year, my father laughed so hard I was silenced.'

Mili learns difference. 'Those poor ambitions of mine were tethered to white liberal visions, norms and privileges.' Her normal is to be constantly conscious of or 'tethered to disparity and negotiated anxieties'. She wants to obey respected academic and author Njabulo Ndebele's entreaty to black thinkers and artists to rediscover the ordinary, but this is hard.

She writes: 'I've been thinking about this idea because I strive to be carefree, I yearn to have a normal existence or just a day where I'm not immersed in a race, gender, class and space dialectic as a fact of my brown life.' In this, Mili is an everywoman and it explains the ubiquity of race in South Africa's national conversation and the annoyance of whites with it. They have always known an insouciant normal; black people are still struggling.

As I delve, I find that until all people are free, until there is not significant social justice, black identification with black suffering (race, gender and class), the black middle and professional strata does not feel itself as one apart from the broader mass. In India, where I have worked with young professionals, and in East Africa, the ability to disaggregate is much clearer and seemingly easier.

At a café in Linden, Mili notes a table of Jewish business people crowded around two teacups – one dusty pink, the other minty green. She eavesdrops. They are manufacturers, deciding on the final production line. It is worth quoting her reflection in its entirety for it contains a wisdom that helps explain why there is no new normal in South Africa's diversity.

'Pure green jealousy settled inside me at the thought that these grown white men had the luxury of convening a business action about crockery. And that they were probably going to make a lot of money from it. I tried to check the jealousy in me in an effort to understand why it was so buoyant, so relentless.

'If I was going to interpret my surroundings, I had to understand their foundations. The difference between them and me is that they inherited the peace of mind to craft and contemplate teacups on a Wednesday afternoon. I inherited the responsibility of discovering, addressing and solving a race, gender and class disparity I did not create.'

That is a big inheritance of responsibility and I think it sits like an albatross around a generation we have carelessly called born free, as if they were free of the burdens of apartheid. It explains why a generation feels itself still in struggle. It is a generation that has trained its eye on whiteness and white privilege as responsible for its burden. Blacks-only spaces are regarded as still highly necessary.

By my reckoning, the only professional group that broke apart its black and white organisations to create a unified organisation was media leaders.

They dissolved the Black Editors' Forum and the Council of Editors to form the South African National Editors' Forum. As my Twitter respondents pointed out, the Black Lawyers Association still exists. Black associations for investment professionals does too. Black managers have two associations – the Black Management Forum and the Progressive Professionals Forum. Black business has a plethora, including the Black Business Council, NAFCOC and a Black Business Executive Circle. There are associations of black planning professionals, accountants and doctors and they are growing apace for two reasons.

The first is that they are a vigorous lobby for more muscular empowerment policies and to push for the cake to be cut more fairly. The second is that, I believe, their members still experience alienation and marginalisation because they remain a minority in all these spheres yet experience the pressure of being regarded as the bulwark to prize open the doors of opportunity for black people in their numbers at the commanding heights of the economy.

Surveying the rage on my timeline upon asking what might have happened if someone organising a #ForWhiteGirlsOnly function had advertised for a speaker, I wonder, 'Am I going mad?' It's a feeling of being out of step, adrift, of being mentally out of touch with the mood of the times that provokes the research of this book.

After searching and reading and travelling from Black Consciousness to class consciousness, I settled on the understanding of non-racialism as the correct path and future for the beloved country. I covered the golden age – from 1991 onwards – and saw in so many big and small ways the sense and sensibility of unity and non-racialism. I believe(d) that the journey through race to nationhood is happening, that the hegemony is shifting.

In my perception of the world, many of the women who responded, some angrily, rule the world. To name just three:

Simphiwe Dana, who is the soundtrack of an era; Haji Mohamed Dawjee, a former *Mail & Guardian* digital editor and now uber digital marketer; and Nzinga Qunta, a journalist and media intellectual.

They are the pace setters, the cultural-makers and markers. They occupy major opinion and shape mine. Many have top jobs – many have had multiple top jobs. For me, they are the new power. And they have been since I started following the path of a new generation with the *Mail & Guardian*'s *200 Young South Africans You Must Take to Lunch*, which I started with Songezo Zibi (who is now the editor of *Business Day* but had then been a motor industry executive with a huge vision) about seven years ago to track this Generation Freedom that had rapidly come to define what it means to be South African, hip, successful and free.

At *City Press*, it has been an immersion into this world with every week defined by new power, be it in business, entre- preneurship and mostly in celebrity and culture. My cultural boundaries are shaped by the likes of DJ Black Coffee and It girl Minenhle Dlamini; by the music of Nakhane Touré; the art of Mary Sibande; the writing of Milisuthando Bongela and the political analysis of Mondli Makhanya. In business, I am empow- ered by Nedbank's former chairperson Reuel Khoza; by Standard Bank's Sim Tshabalala and the Reserve Bank governor Lesetja Kganyago.

In media, my hero is who it has nearly always been, Khanyi Dhlomo, with Songezo Zibi in a new starring role. In civil society, it is Zackie Achmat, Sekoetlane Phamodi and Sisonke Msimang. In public life, it is Thuli Madonsela, Lindiwe Sisulu, Panyaza

Lesufi and deputy speaker Lechesa Tsenoli. My premier is David Makhura. My mayor is Parks Tau. I also enjoy the youthful vigour that EFF leader Julius Malema and DA leader Mmusi Maimane have brought to our politics.

In other words, my life is defined by and led by black power in all its manifestations and tributaries. From where I sit, blacks are the centre of my gaze in all ways.

And this is why I find our narrative of black disempowerment by whites, of black domination by whites, of black marginalisation by whites, so hard to fathom it makes me feel like I am going stark raving mad. I feel as if I've come up against the power that does not know its name or its influence – it is why I think we need a new Steve Biko for the twenty-first century to hold up a mirror of black ability and beauty to see once again the possible and the potential. But to want that is to hold up a mirror of equal and bitter reflection – non-racialism has died, as a dream and a reality and a motivating force in South African life. What we have coalesced into and around is, at best, a benign multi-racialism and, at worst, a coagulating race war fought in the digital ether where black and white seek lives that are separate and striving towards equality.

———

'No. It's not.' I'm snappy with the young man. He has declared, 'Non-racialism means we don't see race.' It means the opposite. I'm no expert, but I know our constitutional principle of non-racialism does not mean we are striving for a race-blind society. It's not simple *Simunye* and nor is it the dreamscape of beer-guzzling, braaing mates standing around a fire that is the narrative of so much feel-good advertising.

I wish it was. I'm like a crotchety old aunty with young people on this topic. I always irritably swat away their understanding. But it is remarkable to me that the only communities even saying the word in my view are usually white people and the older activists allied to the governing ANC and broader liberation movements. That they have entirely the wrong end of the stick is endlessly frustrating but at least they haven't retreated behind the new laagers of white groups on Facebook led by people such as Sunette Bridges, who was the first person found guilty by the Human Rights Commission of violating racial harmony on her page. I have white friends who call themselves 'post-racial', but who don't have any black friends, except me and maybe two others. Their definition of being post-racial, I think, means listening to Karen Zoid, reading Max du Preez and liking Laugh it Off T-shirts.

Zelda la Grange is a figurehead of this progressive strand of Afrikaans speakers and she is the woman who came to embody the accommodation with and inclusion of whites in the transition when she became the trusted aide of Khulu, her name for Nelson Mandela. In late 2014 and early 2015, she found herself on either edge of the fractious barometer of what the relative role of whites is in a free South Africa.

When Zelda published the delightful and best-selling book *Good Morning, Mr Mandela* she faced a storm, notably from Madiba's daughter, Makaziwe Mandela, who said Zelda had no right to produce this inner-circle piece of work on her 19-year relationship with the world's greatest statesperson. On Twitter and Facebook, it went further. How dare a white person write a book about a black person? It matters not that Zindzi Mandela points out her dad had given the thumbs-up to two other books by two security guards.

A few months later, Zelda was at the centre of a storm again. This time for a string of tweets and a Twitter handle change to Zelda van Riebeeck. For a few days, South Africa stood still to shout at Zelda for saying:

- ❏ Makes white people really feel welcome in SA. I think I'm calling [Jan] today to ask him what de hell he was thinking sailing to SA
- ❏ Oh I'm going to ask Pres Hollande [of France – Zelda is of French-Huguenot stock] if he wants me because the organisation that praises Mugabe but condemns De Klerk doesn't want us in SA
- ❏ Yes De Klerk was the last apartheid President and gave in under pressure. But he could have held onto power = civil war

I was momentarily astounded at Zelda's lack of historical rigour. For South Africans, Jan van Riebeeck is not a friendly *oom* but the first of the colonial overlords who began the experiments with land theft and abuse of the original inhabitants that culminated in grand apartheid. How could she not know this?

F.W. de Klerk is, for me, not a heroic figure who bestowed

our freedom upon us. He is a politician who knew how to read the cards right and feel the winds of change and the growl of the *toyi-toyi* from across the country as the United Democratic Front (UDF) and its shock troops made his South Africa thoroughly ungovernable.

What Zelda's tweets also reveal is the often ambivalent patriotism of white people evinced in books with titles such as *Ways of Staying* and wringing-hand websites – should I go or should I stay? What astounds me more is that three tweets could come to define the South African national conversation. How can a young white woman with a poor sense of history despite her proximity to its finest son and statesman do that? A friend answers the question. 'Because we thought she was different.' I prod her. Zelda, she says, is one of the few prominent whites who embodied a sense of Ubuntu. Now it's splattered, like a broken egg. A thin film of trust has been violated.

———

My understanding of non-racialism is that it is the long, hard road through race consciousness to non-racial consciousness where we begin to understand each other as fellow human beings. It is not only a social construct, but a political and economic one, too. It embodies empowerment and equity policies with it in that you can't have one without the other. And, so, our Constitution makes provision for the fix-it policies that will bring it to fruition. One day. Being non-racialist means holding a close understanding of the intergenerational impacts of apartheid. And doing something about them. And it also means holding a vision of a diverse country that can see beyond the respective melanin levels of its varied inhabitants. I hold onto it fervently.

And sometimes it feels like my nine friends and I are the only ones who do. I am dying a little inside upon hitting the Wits campus. My armoury of choice is a yellow T-shirt with Steve Biko called Bikool. It's rubbish pop culture but I need all the help I can get.

A colleague journalist, Vukani Mde, had written a column in *The Daily Maverick* (the platform that is the high road in the digital race war) slating any critique of his decision to wear party apparel to an ANC assembly as the ravings of a 'White Internet', ignoring all the black people who had also thought his actions as a journalist were ethically dubious and certainly partisan. 'White', it felt, had become a pejorative word that silenced views you didn't agree with.

Until 2015 and this incident, it had been generally accepted that journalists should not be card-carrying members or activists for a political party as that can harm perceived and real independence. Vukani wrote defending his decision to wear ANC regalia to the party's meeting on 8 January in Cape Town. Many colleagues (I was one) differed in our opinion; but a growing number agree with the right to take political sides.

I wrote a column called 'White Internet. #WTF' and raised the vision of non-racialism and national unity I hold dear. For that, I got a firestorm. I wear rose-coloured spectacles and sing 'Kumbaya', said those who disagree with me. The debate was hosted by Eusebius McKaiser on Facebook. In it, I come across as an Uncle Tom and naive on top of it. It is painful. It's true that I sing 'Kumbaya' and wear rose-tinted spectacles but it's still death-defying when the big wigs of the black journalism fraternity tell you it is so and that it is completely ignorant, dated and, well, plain stupid. The panel on media and race caught the tailwind of that fracas. Thus, my armoury.

The panel (de)generated into a discussion of race in society. The consensus at that liberal signpost: whites were still in charge; racism was worse than ever and a glum agreement with the brightest person in the room who declared us to be living in a time of white supremacy.

I disagreed. And posited the positives on the way to non-racialism. How many black middle-class people there are (a healthy smattering of whom were in the room), how we have bought things and helped our families and so buoyed our country and economy. How the cities are filled with people of different cultures and races just getting on with getting on.

I spoke about the new establishment and how I understand it. It was like whispering in the wind. Again, I am Uncle Tom, and the house consensus is clear – we are in an era of heightened racial and systematic oppression. I can't believe that at the place, Wits, where I learnt non-racialism, I am in a gathering that has turned its back on the philosophy completely.

In fact, the entire country has done so. There is not a single national campaign, programme or policy that seeks to reach a twenty-first-century understanding of what it means to be a non-racialist in South Africa. The Ahmed Kathrada Foundation has built itself on support for realising a non-racial vision but its campaigns are more anti-racist in nature. Wearing non-racial colours now is like wearing an ill-fitting suit. It is pinned uncomfortably between white race-blindness and the fact that blackness is currency.

There is one question that never gets answered: Okay, so what have you done about it? And what will you do? This is not grand apartheid where there was no means to an ending. There is armoury beyond slogan and T-shirt. The Human Rights Commission, The Commission for Conciliation, Mediation and Arbitration. Joining a trade union. Establishing a staff forum. Agitating. Mobilising. Complaining where it counts and outside of the echo chamber. Because I grew up in a Bolshy generation, I feel the absence of acting about your unhappiness: forming a union or staff association; being part of a movement; taking injustices to the numbers of forums available to us. Tweeting is often insufficient.

We are stuck in this awkward era of being oppressed by an ephemeral and shifting concept of whiteness and intra-racial spaces – an era about as far from the constitutional dream as I could have imagined.

This book is my effort to put the rose-tinted glasses back on, but I do so with a far more nuanced sense of how far we have to go. Apartheid may well have been a blip in the greater path of world history – but there is a generation that feels it has not gone away. I don't agree. But that doesn't matter; the perception is entrenched, parcelled neatly and passed from one generation to the next.

4

A NUMERICAL MAJORITY AND A CULTURAL MINORITY?

It was 2003, nine years into freedom. At the SABC, handsome young man meets beautiful young woman. They bond. The man tells the story of what happens.

'Post '94 our parents got excited and decided to move into the suburbs and all that and left the township,' says Tiyani Rikhotso, who was then an energetic young reporter at the SABC in parliament.

'Me, I never brought a girlfriend home until I was sure she was the person I was eventually going to have a child with in future,' he says explaining his old-school values at odds with the young suburban people he grew up with.

'So, the lady I was dating in Cape Town wanted me to meet her parents because she believed we were getting somewhere. I was 22, 23. She was probably 19 or 20, an intern from Stellenbosch University. At first, she thought I was coloured, but then she told her mother, "No, actually, he's more African from rural Limpopo living in Gauteng." The whole CV had to be laid out.'

Thus it was that Tiyani belted down the N2 in an SABC Conquest. Destination: Stellenbosch; to meet the folks.

'We met at a mall. I wasn't comfortable because she had

hinted that her father was a very conservative Afrikaner. I had asked her to come there early so we could have a conversation before the most uncomfortable meeting of my life. She got there in her own car because she was 19 years old and had a driver's licence.

'I wanted to leave at some stage because I was uncomfortable. She had said to me don't be surprised if my father starts speaking in Afrikaans and all of that, and what have you. I said, "Okay, I think I can match him a bit because I speak some Afrikaans."

'They got there. Sat. It was the father, the mother and younger sister. And then we sat, got introduced to the mother with a smile, politely reached out with her hand. Then, the father shakes my hand as well. It was very cold and very brief. I didn't even feel his hand, in fact. It's as if we did a Wi-Fi handshake. Sorry, a Bluetooth handshake. This is a remote and technical interaction without human warmth or Ubuntu, a spirit of communal meeting.

'It was a typical handshake. I didn't even feel his veins, didn't feel anything. So the mother fired first – she wanted to break the ice because she knew her husband. So she wanted to know, oh so what do you do, wanted to know my family background, you know the typical Q&A that a normal parent would ask whether you are white or black. But, of course, for me, coming from where I was coming from and my understanding of black versus white relations, I felt it was an interrogation. And the father looked quite red. And then he started talking about the SABC, saying it was an extension of the ANC. (I asked him why.) You know why, because the chairperson of the SABC board was a black person. And then we started chatting and I think he said about a paragraph. We sat there for about an hour and a half to two but I can reduce what he said to a paragraph. Half the time he was having a conversation with his wife or with his child.

'You could tell from his face, he was there to tell me: "Nigger, back off."

'When she got to work on Monday, she was very unhappy, she actually broke down. She started relating the [tongue] lashings she got. How culturally uncomfortable he was and what have you … He changed it to make it my problem. He's the one refusing to accept me but he turned the tables to look as if it's going to be my family who says, "Oh, white woman. What for? Why not marry within?"'

His friend, Mayihlome Tshwete, who is around as the story is told, pipes up: 'Your family would have loved it, m'chana.'

Tiyani continues: 'So eventually he made it clear to her he doesn't approve of me and all of that. And the mother had to join the chorus. Why would she want a complicated relationship? And then I called if off, because I just didn't want to …'

Tiyani leaves it hanging there. Later he does date a white English woman. 'It became a political cause for me. I became a Steve Biko after that and just had anger in me. I dated her to prove a point. The looks, the stares you get – you go to Kenilworth. I dated to show them that things have changed currently.'

Tiyani looks like a supermodel. He is kind. Funny. Wickedly smart. Any thinking, potential in-law had to see this, I think. If I had a daughter who brought him home, I would go gaga and think 'son-in-law material'.

But that appalling one and a half hours he spends at a cold-hearted Stellenbosch mall being scrutinised and made to feel as if he is not good enough and his relating of it alters my understanding of where we are in South Africa, race wise. It helps me to grasp why a generation is so angry. That man could string together no more than a paragraph of words to say to the amusing and erudite young journalist who had a thousand young stories to tell.

What Tiyani saw reflected back at him was the view that he didn't match up simply because he had more melanin than the Stellenbosch man. To have your hand shaken as if you are an untouchable is an awful experience anywhere, but imagine its impact when you are a young, up-and-coming, newly freed black South African – the uhuru generation enjoying the first years of a wonderful democracy. It must have been like a slap with a damp rag on a beautiful summer day. And it can turn love to hate, making a mockery of the notion of reconciliation, which, to be frank, was always about black people extending the hand, not the other way around.

South Africa is covered in a patchwork quilt of a million indignities like this that have come to define the experience of a generation of young black people who, I think, are no longer Mandela's children. They may love our founding president, but they do not accept his legacy of peace and reconciliation among races because of the too many times they have been made to feel inferior and subordinate by old privilege and prejudice.

We all know or see enough mixed-race couples and children to know what happened to Tiyani in that mall is not our only story. As an avaricious consumer of such love stories, I can recite many that would make your eyes burn with sentimentality, or in my case, joy. But in my research I've come to know now that the happy rainbow world I believed was a more generalised experience is a tiny contented spot in a vortex of different and painful ones where the hard work of reconciling to life in a country run by a formerly oppressed majority has not been done.

———

The third round table is an exploration with people who have state and political power. You've met Tiyani. With him at an elucidatory dinner we hold is Khusela Sangoni, a beautiful young spokesperson for the ANC. She is also an adviser to the powerful ANC secretary general Gwede Mantashe.

My experience of her is of a thoughtful person.

Once when I was reprimanded for a speech I had made by the ANC high command at Luthuli House on my birthday, and after I had taken along a cake to lighten the meeting, Khusela was the only person on the ANC's side of the table who looked discomforted. I know she arranged for a peace pipe to be smoked with me.

The deputy director general of communication services at Home Affairs, Mayihlome Tshwete, is the stylish face of a new generation of young cadres in the state. Erudite and argumentative, he loves a good fight and is in many ways the perfect son of his luminary father Steve Tshwete, who was also a media darling.

He immediately thinks the title of my book is a play on that trope that South Africa won't survive without whites. 'You know where the question leads you: if it wasn't for whites, you wouldn't have the type of infrastructure we have now.'

It's the furthest thing possible from my thinking, but it's interesting that it is the first destination in Mayihlome's mind. I know the narrative he thinks I intend to mimic: that apartheid was not *that* bad because we have First World infrastructure. It's a popular race narrative among whites, coloureds and Indians, but it's rubbish, of course. Apartheid infrastructure and spatial planning is still costing us enormously in the fractured design of the country and our intractable Group Areas. The 1913 Land Act. Homelands. Black spots.

It's one reason we are where we are.

'No, that's not what I'm saying,' I tell Mayihlome.

He says: 'But the question leads you to that direction. A lot of white people in South Africa believe they have ownership over civilisation. So they're like, "Sure, we made apartheid, we oppressed you. But if it were not for us you wouldn't be wearing that fancy suit." White [Western] civilisation is the only one that has tried to monopolise its contribution to progress.

'Black South Africans, including the ANC, have been put in this position where you chase gradual progress and don't rattle the boat too much because you don't want people to leave and pull out their money.'

A new generation is questioning the fundamental pillars of the South African transition. 'Look, we've flirted with this reconciliation thing. We dated across colour lines at some stages in our lives. We have tried to balance things out but there is just this stubbornness on the part of the majority of white people who refuse to change to the extent that 21 years into democracy, they still feel like they're doing me a favour.'

We couldn't do certain things back then, says Tiyani. 'Now I think we misread the commitment we got from the other side. When we said we will compromise politically, they were to compromise economically, [but did not].

'If there are no whites, we probably wouldn't have to justify as much as we do, trying to create a better life for all our people.'

———

The three, who are at the coalface of the politics of justification, reel off the good policies they must justify. These include BEE, the payment of 16.4 million social grants and, because the issue is burning when we meet, e-tolls.

This culture of justification is one I know well. In my experience, it can result in having to deny who you are and how you got where you are. I speak publicly a great deal and often to diverse groups of women. It is a wonderful adjunct to my daily work of stringing words together to create meaning. These groups are often freedom's fruit – women who are being quickly accelerated because of the pressure exerted on a patriarchal space by laws meant to give meaning, purpose and life to our constitutional principle of non-sexism.

My experience of becoming editor (of the *Mail & Guardian*)

is that black people will often need black sponsors to get where they want to go – if it had been left to white colleagues, my own dream job would not have been achievable because of biased perceptions about me. The political context created by the Constitution and employment equity laws made millions of us visible for racial power tends to replicate itself as it views competence in its own image.

I love those laws and will defend them before any number of civil society groups comprised to fight them in public and in court. I go toe to toe with conservatives such as the author Anthea Jeffrey whose book on black empowerment is, in my opinion, an abomination that deserves to be exploded by a black scholar of empowerment. My badge of 'employment equity candidate' is worn proudly. But I wear it alone.

In all my talks, when I ask the question of who sees themselves as an employment equity candidate, a beneficiary of a good and progressive law, there are uncomfortable silences and much twitchiness. Nobody catches my eye. Maybe a woman or two will put up her hand, hesitatingly, because my silence and waiting for an answer makes the moment uncomfortable. You hold your arm down near your chest, not thrust up proudly in the air. It breaks my heart each time this happens, and it happens every time.

Who did this to us? Who made a laudable process the equivalent of an embarrassing branding? It is the conservatives in our society who have captured the democratic and constitutional narrative about empowerment and turned it against its millions of beneficiaries who will not claim it. How deeply sad this is.

And how powerful are the conservative forces that have deigned numerous times to tell me that I am not an affirmative action candidate because I keep slaying their red herrings.

—

The South African story is a parallel one. For black people who have benefited from freedom (and for those in government), the story is one of accomplishment. Creating a working state from the destructive embers of apartheid's divisive one has been a phenomenal achievement by any measure. But it is seldom a story given sufficient credit in our dominant narrative because there is another narrative.

The second narrative is the story of loss. Of course, there are many liberal and progressive white people who are onside the democratic project, but the narrative of a people who have lost power remains a shaping force in society.

The transition from apartheid to a democratic system required nimble footwork to get the co-operation of the security forces as well as the nervous white population. Guaranteeing property, land and certain group rights were key to this endeavour. If you read Afrikaans media, you will detect that land and property rights and the debates about them are topics that make many whites skittish. The lobby to ensure their protection is loud, powerful and increasingly vehement as the government floats more radical ideas about land and the expropriation of property.

Because of the structure of private media and the arrangement of lobbies, the minority and property rights camp is more influential than the lobby for more muscular land expropriation – Julius Malema and the EFF are changing this pattern, though. The malfunctioning state (symbolised by a ramshackle power supply, a constant feed of stories of state hospitals falling apart and people dying, and the rate of exodus from public to private schools) is also a lobbying point for a conservative white population.

South Africa has privileged one story (of a loss of power and of dysfunction) over the other story – of rapid social mobility and a better life. Inevitably, the two stories take on a racial hue.

This knowledge of the power of the anti-narrative means similar trends in society resonate with me even as my three fellow discussants rail against them.

Mayihlome comments: 'When my phone rings, I'm not answering to the people who voted the ANC into government. I'm answering a white guy who says there are potholes at the Home Affairs office in Randburg. Tiyani's answering to white guys about e-tolls. I'm answering to immigration guys, European people, who want to travel into South Africa without passports. When you go to Europe, you give them your fingerprints, your eye scans, everything. No problem. But when they come here, it's, "Why do I have to do that to go to South Africa?" So, it's a devaluation of South Africa.'

I prod. But why does it matter that much? Why do you justify so much?

Khusela: It's the standards that white people set …
Ferial: Is that their power?

Khusela: The standards that white people set tend to be the norms that people believe we must follow. Take a knife and fork. I have a lot of friends, especially Pedi people, who eat with their hands. But now I've been socialised in a particular way, where I get uncomfortable, where even if my Indian friends chow curry and rice with their hands, I'll think, 'Can't she use a fork and knife?' But, honestly, the standards are set by white people. It's an aspirational culture.

Ferial: But can you decide to change it?

Khusela: It's difficult to define yourself outside of that mode because that is what is regarded as acceptable because the culture we've assimilated is not necessarily the standard we would have defined.

Ferial: Why is your identity and a sense of self so predicated on what white people think?

Tiyani: Because that is where we come from, that is the past we come from.

I know Khusela, Mayihlome and Tiyani to be powerful people who are agenda-setters and exemplars of a generation.

'What I want to talk about,' I say to them as we sit down in dialogue, 'is that the transfer of power is far more profound and far more primary than our narrative seems to understand. You set the media agenda far more than your public statements suggest.'

In other words, I want to ask them – why do you sometimes make yourself sound powerless when you are powerful?

'I agree. Case closed,' says Mayihlome, laughing and making it clear he does not agree. 'If you say to me I control the agenda, I want to have a discussion about a number of the good things that are happening in the country. [But] the current context is that we are highly pessimistic and our level of analysis is quite weak.'

Khusela feels herself as being part of a force that is counter-hegemonic – that she is in opposition to a dominant authority even though she is the face of a governing party running South Africa with a huge majority. Like previous people I've spoken to, Khusela buys into the theory of black people being a numerical majority and a cultural minority. She says: 'I totally disagree [with you] on the large extent to which South Africa has moved.'

White people, as a group, are of declining social importance and, in my view, black influencers give this white group more power than it has, so creating a vicious circle. But, challengingly for me, the three associate the media closely with white corporate and financial power. For Mayihlome, the worlds where whites hold sway set the agenda and this lends an amplifying effect.

'There [are] two sets of power,' says Tiyani, adding, 'I know there is power when I go into a meeting of the top six of the ANC. But when I walk out, I don't feel the same way.

'I was listening to 702 and this guy called in … basically, he said black people must be educated first before they can have ambition of running businesses and big corporates …' (To Tiyani it sounds like the qualified franchise idea bandied about by white liberals who advocated giving a certain class of black and coloured people a limited enfranchisement.)

'It brought a particular point home for me in that it said, in fact, we're at ransom here. Yes, we have our power, we contest elections, we get 65%, we get 63.5% [62%] and all of that, and here is a group [which is] very, very small in size, which controls capital in South Africa.'

I ask, 'Do you still think whites control all capital?'

And Tiyani replies: 'They do because if you look at the empowerment interventions we have tried [to implement] they have not really changed the balance of forces.'

Two things strike me in our conversations. While Ukhozi FM and all of the SABC's different language radio stations attract huge black audiences, as do the commercial behemoths such as Metro FM and 5FM, it is what is said on 702 (a smallish station with a mixed listenership but one that has historically catered to the northern suburbs of Johannesburg where rich people live) that figures much more largely in the ranking of agenda by the young people I meet here.

'Your 702s, your *Sunday Times*, we fund them [by way of advertising in and on them]. If 702 calls and a community radio station calls, I'm thinking, Eish! They're going to think my boss [Home Affairs minister Malusi Gigaba] is an idiot if I don't do 702.'

The second thing that strikes me is the view that all money or capital is white when any number of studies will reveal that is not so. It's a stubborn perception across black South Africa and I realise again just how successful what we used to call 'apartheid capitalism' was. But it sets up fundamental complexities for South Africa and a new South African economy if money is regarded as whiteness. South Africa in business has more than a little work to do to change this perception, as has our governing party, which directly and indirectly controls a lot of capital, but spending patterns have often been inefficient or, in certain cases, created elite patterns of new capital consumption or accumulation.

And, again, I find that the individual lives of people, no matter how much they have been reshaped by freedom, matter little in how they understand change or how they see the significant tapestry woven in a new South Africa.

Take this exchange.

Tiyani comments: 'We are being forced to live in 84-square-metre houses with our families. That can't be [the] power [you speak of]. Where's the land for us to build the sizeable house where our children can play around the same way white kids play in the suburbs.'

Earlier, Tiyani had said he lives in a complex with enough lawn for children to play. So, I ask about his Fourways home: 'But your life isn't lived in 84 square metres?'

'But my uncle in Orlando West lives in a back room.'

I ask Tiyani if freedom will only have arrived properly once his uncle has a home like his?

The theme is one this book's path has helped me to discern. You can't disaggregate middle-class black people's experience of freedom from the wider black community's. It is a mistake I have made repeatedly, which is to tally the black middle class as an example of freedom at work because there are now roughly equal numbers of black and white middle-class people. For me, this felt like a milestone for the democratic state – a measuring up, and a successful one at that.

But the under-class, the left-behind is still too high and it is not a notional under-class – a thing of a distant national solidarity. It's your mom, your dad, your uncle, your brother, sister, nephew …

Until there is a more generalised sense of well-being and realisable aspirations, the discourse won't shift – until there is a better social justice system now and hope in the future.

Mayihlome explains why this is the case. 'I have got cousins who stay in the rural area. When they don't have money, they call me. When they have another kid, they call me. When that kid grows up and wants to start going to school, they call me. Or they call my mother. So our financial burdens, as guys living in Fourways, are not the same. Tiyani staying in Fourways compared to a white guy staying in Fourways [is] not the same. The white guy's poorest cousin may be the kid trying to start a band on a penny. Our poorest cousins are people who are asking us for R350.00 to survive the month.'

Colloquially called a 'black tax', this phenomenon of an emerging middle class squeezed by family and community obligations is becoming an omnipresent theme of black urban life. On Facebook, you can read serial accounts of the ways in which black professionals, like myself and like the young people I am speaking to, are stuck with living up to a set of aspirations while also ensuring they do not leave behind cousins, cousin-brothers, sisters, nieces, nephews, friends and, of course, older parents who place great store in a first generation of made-its.

The pressure feels combustible sometimes and contributes to what I see as a burbling rage in compatriots who live the bifurcated existence of the liberated and thrusting-forward cadre who is constantly, painfully reminded of how many have been left behind.

Like most black spots, the one where I grew up had its fair amount of racial measuring. People with nicer homes and cars were 'living like whites'. Keeping to yourself and not playing street games earned you the insult of 'thinking you're white'. Straightening your hair (and sometimes your tie) and being fair enough to get on the better buses or evade the train inspector in certain coaches was 'passing for white'.

——

Tiyani rises to my theme. 'What if there were no whites in South Africa? What if there had never been a Union of South Africa? What if John Dube [a legendary founding president of the ANC] had been president of South Africa? We wouldn't have these conversations. We wouldn't be playing this catch-up game that we are trying to play now because of the apartheid system that approached development from a racial point of view, where it was good for her to receive an inferior education while her racial counterpart of the same age probably with the same potential to be great went to a different school where a different level of education was offered. So we wouldn't be dealing with all this that we are dealing with currently.'

And, then, he throws in this for good measure. 'If there would be no whites, Ferial, I would be Koos Bekker [on my way to being Koos Bekker].'

If South Africa, and Africa, has a media magnate, he is Koos Bekker, now chairperson of Naspers and the man who took an Afrikaans media newspaper group and turned it into a global media company, making himself and many others a fortune based largely by timing digital disruptions perfectly.

It's interesting that Tiyani starts his narrative with John Dube, who was also one of the country's first editors, and ends it with Bekker – as if the one had to have his ambitions nixed for the other one to rise.

For Khusela: 'If there were no whites, we probably wouldn't have to justify as much as we have to, trying to create a better life for all our people ... our starting point is always having to appease.'

> *Ferial: Like how?*
>
> *Khusela: Okay, let's speak about BEE, grants. Grants are a perfect one. Because you now have a narrative that has developed in society from a people who are a minority saying only few of us work and we have to pay 16 million people blah, blah, blah. I don't think that narrative has developed from black South Africa, neh?*
>
> *Ferial: All of us (working black people and all consumers because we all pay value-added tax) pay taxes and, by and large, we do so happily. So why don't you control that narrative? There are now more tax-paying black South Africans than white ones.*

The answers highlight a narrative that isn't sufficiently well explored in our public life. Capital, or money, or value, is still, largely, perceived as being in the control of an amorphous group of whites, despite evidence to the contrary.

I think it's because workplaces have not shifted sufficiently to provide an image or a mirror that shows money and financial power have also changed hands. But here is what my fellow discussants feel.

> *Tiyani: Who employs Ferial (me)? Who is in charge of industry currently in South Africa? Mining, telecoms, property?*
> *Ferial: MTN, for example, is owned and run by black people.*
> *[For what it's worth, I am employed by the shareholders of Naspers and by the board of Media24, which is led by black economist and mathematician Rachel Jafta. I also hold a few BEE shares in MTN and so read their documents with extreme care.]*
> *Mayihlome: How is MTN black people?*

I don't know what to say here because MTN factually is black-owned and I want to move the conversation on. MTN is the best example of black success. Starting with the granting of a licence to a group of visionary black shareholders, MTN is the finest example of how to do empowerment. But its story is not well known.

In fact, the stories of big black successes that have made tectonic shifts in the economic landscape are not known, which opens vast questions in my mind: as a journalist, what have I

111

been doing if not writing about these so that a young man like Mayihlome better knows the story of our recent economic empowerment history, which is small but significant.

As a young person growing up in the hopeful 1990s, I saw the future as pegged differently – as if Mzansi would be a black Scandinavia, an African social democracy. There would be lots of great public housing and public transport; exceptional public health. A peoples' democracy had me imagining public halls where public servants would hold counsel and referendums. Those are the things of the young imagination I still hold dear – but they are incredibly dated for a new generation, which pegs its aspirations and measures itself by the life and style and culture of a tiny minority of post-colonial elites.

Perhaps the reason I don't *get* the whiteness studies and the nascent discourse of South Africa gripped by a white supremacy is because we were taught differently in political organisations. The vision of a new South Africa was never to live like whites or to have privilege like a post-colonial elite – it was to make a different society.

Simple calculations will show it's never going to happen – all black people are never going to have a 'white' lifestyle and neither is it what my generation understood our striving to be for.

Not for the first time in the shaping of my ideas for this book do I feel dated like a yellowing UDF poster – a hippy relic of a time when the future looked so different. But if this writing and research process has taught me anything, it is that we need new imaginations to think of what a different, good society would look like.

So, my ears perk up when Khusela muses: 'Tiyani made the point that's been made all the time that as much as the struggle was not about living like white people, the reality is you would want to have the same economic opportunities and be able to have the same benefits.'

So, I ask: 'What is living like white people?' – a measure I still hear bandied about.

> *Mayihlome: It's financial security.*
>
> *Khusela: Financial security. I aspire to Patrice Motsepe [one of Africa's richest men and a mining magnate]. There's an aspirational sense in the black community – I mean, if I get a new car, it will be a new car like* mlungu. *It smells like a white person.*
>
> *Mayihlome nails it: White isn't race, it's wealth.*
>
> *Tiyani: It's about financial security. When my boss annoys me, I also want to throw my toys around, go to flying school, whatever. Everything that's respectable and admirable is so defined. My gardener calls me* mlungu.

An advance, an improvement, an aspiration is defined as white – how much work we have to do! And what displacement has been suffered.

With the black dependence on income (as opposed to wealth), you can't chuck it up and go to flying school. There is little that is carefree about being black and middle class given the political and financial responsibilities of not only my three fellow discussants but of a full generation.

113

———

There is an entire world of white privilege that was invisible to me and that was made visible only once I integrated into it – my first collision was at university. With a generation of young black people, this is happening much sooner at school now. At Wits, I was perplexed that all the white students had cars. How the hell was that possible, I remember 18-year-old me, belched from a yucky Putco bus in Braamfontein, asking myself.

Cars. When you get them. And how you learn to drive them could be a whole book on their own. My dad learnt to drive because his factory-owner employer needed someone to lock up the factory. And, so, by default, we had a small delivery car. I grew up with having a car parked at the open parking underneath our block of flats, but the cars were always headaches. Often they were second hand. They were always in the backyard of a neighbourhood mechanic and barely got my mom and dad to work.

My first car came when I got a job at a university library. It cost me R5 000 paid in instalments; and R25 000 in repairs until a kind boyfriend said, 'Give it up, Fer.' I recognised my luck later when among the intake of *Weekly Mail* trainees I was the only one with *that* car, which took us about when it wasn't stuck. And I guess it's because I grew up coloured and my father's pitiful wages were more than the average black worker.

So, how 18-year-olds could afford brand-new cars was an absolute mystery to me until I learnt of the privileged rituals of many of my white compatriots' lives, which were unbelievable and are still unrecognised as factors of catapulting privilege in how we understand South Africa.

They got dropped and fetched at school. They got braces to fix dental imperfections (this was a real learning curve for me as the only time I got taken to someone I still consider a horse dentist was when things were really sore). They had extra tuition if needed. University was not the hit and miss of my generation (very few of us at my secondary school made it to university) but a thing of certainty. They went on overseas holidays. Every year. Their families had second homes. This one really hit me in the gut as a kid whose parents didn't own a home until 1987 when my brother could pitch in. Two houses!

After university, you could take a gap year. The only thing I would have got is a gap tooth if my plans were not to find work immediately after university. Truth be told, I had to work all the way through university as everything from shop assistant to a butcher to pay my own way. So, a gap year? No such.

When you marry, you get a deposit on a home. There is often a trust fund and bequeathals to grandchildren. This passage of wealth through the generations is a massive failsafe in an uncertain world. The networks of privilege enable easy access into the private sector or the world of the entrepreneur. They continue to smooth lives and careers, creating access and opportunity.

When I finally earned enough to make a will, the consultant asked me about a trust fund? I stared blankly and only after she explained did I learn what all the estate planning I read about in personal finance pages was about. Again, it was a rude wake-up call to the lingering impacts of racial capital in South Africa and to all I did not take for granted.

All of this natural white privilege is almost completely foreign to black people coming into a white world – save for a small and happily growing part of upper middle-class black South Africans.

——

If my response was that of disbelief and a tinge of envy, if I am to be honest, for a new generation of young black people who collide with all they don't have much sooner than my generation did, the response is furious.

When black fury meets white denial, you have the combustible and fundamentally changed race relations we live in today.

#OpenStellenbosch is a students' movement to alter power relations at Stellenbosch University. It exploded into national consciousness through a documentary called *Luister* launched on YouTube.

It was an excoriating account of the experiences of black students both on campus and off. A powerful documentary, it was followed by a week of enhanced activism as the nation sat up and listened to deeply worrying accounts of students' pain at a language policy that continued to favour Afrikaans speakers although the academy is officially bilingual, with English as the second language.

Off campus, students said they faced overt racism in social

and commercial relationships: who you can dance with; where you can eat; and how many black people are allowed into spaces.

It feels as if the harsh reality a young Tiyani encountered has not shifted in 12 years. The harsher reality is the documentary was made 21 years after apartheid ended. Ended. Now there's a complex concept, because did it? Really?

Because pretty and quaint Stellenbosch, with its linked histories of elite Afrikaners and French Huguenot lineage, is possibly one of the most popular tourist spots in South Africa, the story went global. Finally, the black experience was being heard.

To which some white Maties (Stellenbosch students) responded with #WhereIsTheLove, based on the song. Asked to explain, a student who had started the hashtag contra-protest and march said it was all being blown out of proportion and that race didn't matter. He was all long haired, very *bru* and faux hippy, talking Woodstock and the Beatles but without any sense of history or the present. I wanted to cuff him through the TV screen – and could only imagine his denialist impact on a movement finding its voice.

The clash between #OpenStellenbosch and #WhereIsTheLove is a microcosm: people lost in translation to each other with one crew failing to hear properly what the other is trying to tell them.

Tiyani's earlier words come to mind again: '[If there were no whites] ... we wouldn't be playing this catch-up game ...'

———

1994. Long chronicled as a miracle for the bloodshed and pain our negotiators evaded by building relationships and making common ground and common purpose a South African religion, 1994 is splintering and fracturing as it is questioned by a new generation.

Says Tiyani: 'I think we over- or misread the commitment that we got from the other side to say that, as much as they're willing to compromise politically, they are going to compromise economically as well. We over-estimated their commitment to change. We believe that their commitment to change politically also translated to change gradually insofar as economic skills are concerned.

'So, I understand why we had to enter into those negotiations and all those compromises, sunset clauses … [but now] I ask myself was that the best deal we can actually give to the nation?' [He answers 'yes', citing the fear of capital flight.]

Khusela volunteers: 'You see a lot of the issues in South Africa that would be resolved if you felt that white power was trying as much as we are in order to bridge that divide and collectively build our country. I think white people often believe they have a monopoly on just about everything. And we allow them to do that.'

> *Ferial: But how do you experience that in your daily life?*
> *Tiyani: You even have to prove yourself to a plumber …*
> *Khusela: … the plumber comes to your house and you have to*
>   *go there and actually prove the fact that 'actually, this is my*
>   *house and you are working for me'.*

There is a discernible generational shift in how much reaching across race happens and who does it. I feel it myself as a believer in a peaceful coexistence across diversities and that we must reach across and out to each other. This view feels almost archaic, like a relic, as if it is a philosophy that belongs in the Apartheid Museum.

'Can I ask you a question?' Mayihlome asks of the group. 'What's wrong with being disliked by white people? You see, if I asked a young person versus asking an older person you'd get two different answers. Young people, [if you] push them long enough, they'll say, "You know what. I don't give a damn." The elderly will say, "M'chana, chill, let's try to manage things as we need to." And this is the Mandela hangover, right? We still think we're going to get that level of perceived reconciliation.'

It's striking how much reconciliation is regarded as a one-way street – from black to white – as is the building of an inclusive and united society. And for an influential group of people, like the ones I am speaking to, reconciliation and all its attendant philosophies is regarded as an encumbered inheritance not a mantle to wear proudly.

Says Khusela: 'You're stuck in a mentality where you're trying to compromise, you're trying to be inclusive, [aiming for] social cohesion. It's difficult to address it [racism] head on because you have a programme of national reconciliation, nation-building, blah blah blah.'

Blah blah blah. This term perfectly encapsulates how a younger generation feels about the founding democratic pact of South Africa. It's just so much blah blah blah. If, to my generation, 1994 was a signal to a kind of utopia (given where we had come from), for the political millennial, the negotiation to end apartheid resulted in the compromise state, which has become almost a dystopia.

Our race wars are fought in the places of our new privilege. The beautiful restaurants of the Cape are a hotbed of black contestation for the treatment meted out to a new generation of consumers. Why do you put me behind a pole? Did you notice I've been waiting for half an hour? To get a menu.

In one infamous case that still makes me incredulous, a white woman calls and gets a reservation for her black friend. Friend arrives and the restaurant's 'full'. Nobody is fired, when I last checked.

A friend of mine, Sarita Ranchod, writes a double-page spread detailing chapter and verse the everyday indignities of dining in the Cape when black. A woman I barely know, a public relations doyen apparently, thinks it's her place to email me saying: 'How dare you? [report on race and restaurants] Do you know what you're doing?' I'm sure she secures the best reservations and has never been seated behind a pole and left to stare into space as waitrons bustle past to serve someone who dropped in after you.

The online comments sections of news websites are the battlegrounds of our twenty-first-century race war. In September 2015, News24 editor-in-chief Andrew Trench took the brave decision to close comments because he did not want South Africa's premier news site to be host to the worst instincts of our communities.

Gyms are a froth of sweaty race battles as testosteronefuelled white dudes do not want to share the weight of the new South Africa equally. Club land in the Cape is a trusty venue for fisticuffs. In 2015, private schools got hauled into the court of public opinion for language policies that are the new veneer masking racial separation.

The country stands still for a moment, as we do, and shouts at a Curro school when a video appears showing kids emerging from separate buses after a school trip. Nothing odd in that, except the kids in one bus are black; the kids in the other are white.

The Constitution did not enshrine the principle of separate but equal – it encourages us to create non-racial systems. For the first time, parents began to cast a look at their teaching faculty and found few black teachers. Universities, especially those with colonial-era statues, are staging posts of the deferred revolutions of the 1990s as students take on everything from the ideas behind negotiated heritage to curriculum, language and faculty policies.

———

Is it the revolution we didn't have in 1994? Or is it the inevitable racial bumper cars of a middle class crashing into each other's cultures, arm-wrestling each other off turfs as they get used to the idea of the other. Is this what a warts-and-all non-racialism was always going to look like?

This time, Tiyani is in a roaring Golf GTI. It's the sexiest car and if you touch the accelerator, the engine growls. Instant respect. Except if you're black and live in a townhouse complex in northern Johannesburg, apparently. 'There used to be this couple opposite who used to complain about the noise of my car. They put in speed bumps although I never sped. There was a whole long petition.'

Tiyani moved into the complex in 2009 and he lives in a state of fragility with his white neighbours. It is not only his car that has changed since that life-altering tea with the father of a white girlfriend in Stellenbosch – his approach to white people has shifted.

'Given my levels of mistrust of white people, coming from where I was coming from, it became difficult for me to reach out to him.' He is talking about a neighbour who has finally been to visit after they have lived in the same complex for six years. Why had it taken so long? 'It became difficult for me to reach out to a white person who opens his garage door from a hundred metres away so he doesn't have to stop and greet his black neighbour.'

Why had he invited the neighbour over? 'The children play together; the helpers go out and walk them around the estate and they end up playing together. So, we met at my daughter's birthday. "Hi, I'm Mathew", and "Hi, I'm Tiyani." All of that what have you. But, still, man, I'm not feeling this guy and six years later, I'm still not regretting my decisions not to speak to him.'

The suburban clash of cultures can dim the brightest of rainbow nation adherents. Upon moving into Killarney, I desperately wanted to know my neighbours. I wanted to replicate the communal life I'd grown up in – in the houses and kitchens of neighbours who were always 'Aunty' or 'Uncle' and were homes away from home. The alienation of white suburban life is difficult – as difficult as it was for the neighbour whose door I knocked on in Killarney and from whom I asked to borrow an onion.

The man, a well-known northern suburbs fabric designer I often see featured in décor books, looked horrified. 'An onion?' He handed one over with disdain. I gave it back as soon as I could – it had been a ploy to say hello and it failed miserably. It was not the beginning of good neighbourliness, and when he and his partner married from their apartment, I remember watching out of the window and wondering what world I'd landed in where you don't invite your neighbour to your wedding.

Rainbow-nation me is not one to give up, though. At Eid a few years ago, my niece and I thought we would try something similar to get to know our neighbours. We carried over plates of Eid goodies to neighbours who looked, shall I say, dumbfounded and a little suspicious at the gifts. It hasn't broken the ice of suburban life. The other day, an Uber driver who had come to fetch me asked why my neighbour was taking photographs of him.

I have yet to work up the courage to ask her why, as she does the thing Tiyani spoke of – opens her garage from far off, so we don't have to talk.

Race? Or weird? Who knows?

But what I've learnt in my suburban life is that black people don't take their culture with them when they move from township to suburb – because we are still a minority, we are shoehorned into ways that can feel hugely alienating and inculcate simmering resentment. For the longest time, I tried to befriend the neighbour who calls me Muriel but I don't really care any more, like Tiyani no longer does. And when I go over to the woman who thinks it's okay to take photographs of black men in cars, she will get what for.

5

LOOKING AT SOME NUMBERS

Political leaders in our government host many interesting events that I occasionally get to experience. One that catches my eye is the Ecomobility World Festival – a green initiative to get car-loving citizens of Johannesburg to use public transport. It launches on a perfect Sunday morning early in October 2015.

The idea is to walk, cycle, skateboard, Segway or ride from Sandton to neighbouring Alexandra on electric-powered motor-cycles, bikes and, for Transport Minister Dipuo Peters, a little car that looks like a popemobile. I pull on my Nikes and start walking.

It's delightful. Political leaders, such as Johannesburg mayor Parks Tau and Gauteng premier David Makhura, abandon their blue-light convoys to cycle. The starter gun goes off outside the Michelangelo Hotel, which styles itself along Italian Renaissance lines with Corinthian columns and ornate gold. The streets, which usually buzz with gleaming sedans, are quiet as the cyclists and walkers take over.

At a slower pace, the rate of growth in Sandton is quite something to look at. If we are on the edge of a recession, it doesn't show here. Manhattan-style buildings compete for a perch on the ever-changing skyline. Glass vies with concrete as captains of industry take their Sandton buildings higher, greener (allegedly) and as uber-designed as anything in global capitals.

We walk. Past the JSE and a now-disembowelled Village Walk shopping centre. I can't wait to see what will emerge from the crater created by its implosion. This is Joburg. We take things down to build them back up – the city's always been a paean to money and it's no different today.

We pass Nedbank's sprawling headquarters – the green bank has just reported a sterling set of results. Past Rand Merchant Bank, which competes at the top end of the market and owns an HQ that is like a city within a city. Past Discovery, the medical-aid administrator that is successfully exporting its Vitality health rewards system to China and to the United Kingdom.

Down Katherine Street where new hotels sprout, catering to a growing clientele of foreign business people who use Sandton as a base to move into the rest of our continent. Up towards Wynberg, where the economy is older. Manufacturers. Auto workshops. Furniture outlets.

The cops keep the sedans and sport utility vehicles at bay; their drivers look exasperated but resigned – pretty much the look of capital in South Africa, which has made great post-apartheid fortunes but is not terribly highly regarded by the governing ANC.

And then it's up a road and into Alex. A different world. In about six kilometres. The streets are packed with honking Toyota Avanzas, Ses'fikile taxis and private cars. The city fathers give up the effort to keep cars off the road in Alex. The public transport network is too shabby here and the taxis would have a conniption if the bureaucrats try to give the roads over to pedestrians on the first Sunday of the month.

It's a happy and prosperous enough chaos. Chickens ready for slaughter squawk unhappily in their cages. Fresh cow heads are set up six-by-six under a tree, as an outdoor butcher takes a newly sharpened knife to the heads that will later be braaied as Sunday afternoon *shisa nyama*. City workers and professionals do their Sunday chores or eat out at McDonald's, KFC and Chicken Licken that dot the malls that have sprung up over the past 15 years.

Earlier in 2015, Alex went up in violent paroxysms as foreigners were attacked and one, Emmanuel Sithole, was murdered in full view of *Sunday Times* photographer James Oatway's camera and writer Beauregard Tromp's pen. Sithole's slow-motion murder, captured for the world to see, ended the orgy of violence as the state sent in troops.

On this Sunday, some six months later, the place is a peaceful hubbub.

Freedom has been good to Alex, as the honking cars show. There are new additions to the township with a mix of basic and prettier houses, publicly owned flats and a solar geyser roll-out that holds the key to our energy future. Each new house has a geyser on top of it. On a day that is boiling at over 30 degrees by mid-morning, you can understand why solar power is a winner.

Alex is also bursting out of its seams – a rapid click movement of people who migrate from rural areas, settle outside cities and in townships like this one. There are large communities of Zimbabwean and Mozambican people who now call this melting pot home. Houses are built onto the pavements and shacks added to rent out to people who want to be close to work in neighbouring Sandton and surrounds. Orderly development and services such as litter control and road repairs appear to have been abandoned to the abundant smarts of people who call Alex home. Other than the odd cycle lanes we ooh and aah at, there is no sign of any attempt to provide old Alex with at least the basics of municipal public services, such as refuse collection, traffic control and by-law enforcement.

It seems to me on this day that the state finds it easier to regulate and develop the money pot of Sandton – or that capital does so with the excellent improvement district concepts, where public and private sectors come together to create teams that keep up identified spaces so they are safe and nice.

———

This is our story. Pristine next to chaotic. Opulent homes cheek by jowl with shack life. People with too much in a pique of conspicuous consumption who live next door to, but a life apart from, people who can do with more.

I stopped doing the Alex and Sandton comparison because it felt trite and unchanging. And because there are so many similar stories to tell around the country. Diepsloot and Dainfern. Umhlanga and Umlazi in Durban. Llandudno and Lwandle in Cape Town.

It's everywhere, this story of inequality in South Africa that underpins the fury of our race debate. And results in xenophobic attacks, where an 'other' is blamed for the impacts of inequality. Where 'white' describes a good life and having nice things, race is amplified in any understanding of South Africa.

Sandton is no longer only white, but it is largely so. Alex is all-black with few exceptions. When he visited South Africa in October 2015, economist Thomas Piketty, who wrote the book *Capital in the Twenty-First Century* that has put inequality back, front and centre in development economics, noted that race is still a key determinant of wealth.

It is. But it also is not. Here's a different story.

——

For millions of South Africans, freedom has offered significant social mobility at a pace faster than the United States, which prides itself on its ability to move people up the social ladder. The consultancy Futurefact undertook research to ask people where they were on the class ladder compared with their parents.

When I first saw the research, it was my life in a set of bar graphs. In his memoir, *Coolie Come Out and Fight*, my uncle, Mac Carim, tracks the life of our previous generation.

It was a difficult life and clearly one lived too close to the poverty line. In the book, he uses the term 'roses in a dung heap' to describe the life of his wife Hajoo and her sisters Ayesha (my mum), Fatima and Farida, who turned their modest homes into little havens in what we only today recognise as slums.

At family functions Uncle Mac is fond of looking around at

his next generation, which includes sons, nieces and nephews, and marvelling at what freedom has given us – comfort, independence, ambitions and purpose; all of which are the assets of social mobility.

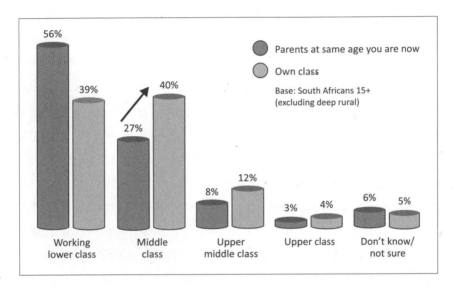

South Africans on the move

Source: Futurefact Survey 2011 in *City Press*, October 2011.

The results of the Futurefact research were fascinating. The number of people who identified as working class (compared with their parents) was much lower. The number of people who identified as middle class was much higher. The number of people who said they did not know was small.

Futurefact's Jos Kuper claims: 'In the US, it takes an average four generations for a poor American family to reach the income of an average family, yet profound change is occurring in the space of one generation in South Africa.' In addition, she found that optimism is high among an older generation. '[About] 56% of parents believe their children's future standard of living when they reach their age will be better than their own.'

This is the opposite to Germany where 73% of parents feel their children would be worse off; one in two Americans concur; while 44% of the French are pessimistic about the decade to come.

But the number of middle-class people grows too slowly, and over the past six years this kind of social mobility has been hobbled by an economy that did not increace at levels significant enough to take it to critical mass.

If you drill down into what we loosely call the middle class in South Africa, it yields further light.

The actual middle class (that is, those people who fall into the middle of the income spread) is relatively low-income. In 2008, these households earned between R1 520 and R4 500 a month.

The relatively affluent middle class earns between R5 600 to R40 000 a month. The elite, defined as those who earn over R40 000 a month, is small, at 4% of the working population.

The actual middle class is overwhelmingly black, while the affluent middle class is more or less divided in half between black and white.

The elite is 60% white and 20% black African. The middle class as a whole is bookended by a tiny number of super-wealthy individuals and a large under-class.

But to assume that these are neat and distinct groups is wrong. There is a deep and umbilical connection between all parts of the black middle class and the poor – funds and dependencies flow from the one to the other.

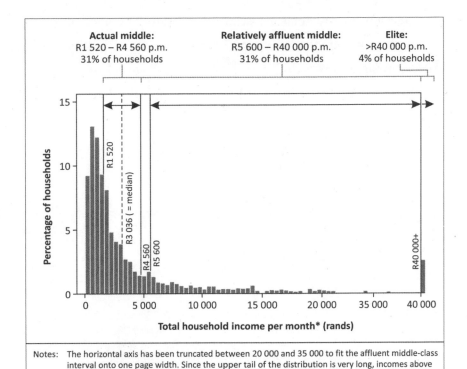

Who is middle class?

Source: Justin Visagie, Econ3x3.

The popular narrative about whites reminds me of Mercator projections of the size of Africa on most maps. In 2010, software and graphic user interface designer Kai Krause caused a stir when he showed how much bigger Africa is in reality. While maps make Greenland and Africa look largely equal in size, our continent is 14 times bigger.

In South Africa, you would swear that whites make up a much larger proportion of the population. In fact, the numbers of whites are in steady decline as many emigrate. The pace of population growth is smaller too. In 1996, there were 31 million black African people here – the 2014 projection was at 43 million.

There were 4.4 million whites in 1996 and there are 4.5 million today.

	1996	2001	2011	2014 Projection
African	76.7% 31 127 631	79.0% 35 416 166	79.2% 41 000 938	80.2% 43 333 700
Coloured	8.9% 3 600 446	8.9% 3 994 505	8.9% 4 615 401	8.8% 4 771 500
White	10.9% 4 434 697	9.6% 4 293 640	8.9% 4 586 838	8.4% 4 554 800
Indian	2.6% 1 045 596	2.5% 1 115 467	2.5% 1 286 930	2.5% 1 341 900
Other	0.9% 375 204	*	0.5% 280 454	*

* Responses in the category 'Other' in 2001 were very few and were therefore imputed. There was no data for this category in the 2014 report. The other figures add to 100% so the assumption is that it was also imputed.

Population statistics in South Africa

Source: Statistics South Africa Census 2011 and subsequent mid-year population projections.

Working on the figure of 43 million black people in South Africa, this means the middle segment is at just over 10% of the total. For South Africa to experience a more comfortable level of black prosperity, you need this class to triple over the medium term.

Another reason the black middle class has not grown substantially is that employment equity is failing at top and senior management levels. The culture of workplaces is set at these levels and South Africa's fragile race relations are often an outcome of such workplaces.

Workplaces are still run on Anglo-Saxon or Afrikaans dominant cultures, and, for a generation of black people, they are deeply alienating environments where blacks check their identities in at the door and where old (white) networks continue to determine who gets ahead and who does not.

By the end of 2014, black top managers still only comprised one in five of the total complement. Senior managers numbered slightly more. Yet, at the professionally qualified and skilled level, the number of black people is much higher at 38.4% and 59.2% of the total respectively. This indicates that black people and women are not breaking through a glass ceiling in the corporate sector.

It hasn't been the purpose of this book to study why this has not happened but clearly it is an area where leaders in society need to knock their brains together to reset workplace cultures and assess how progress can be achieved.

In my experience, what white managers will often label skills deficits are, in fact, network deficits as well as an absence of privileged life 'smarts'. Until I taught myself, I had no idea how to talk to senior managers because nobody in my family had ever had to do so.

As workers, my family was so far down the rung this was neither a learnt nor a required skill. When I was invited to board meetings, my etiquette was a similar blind spot. I can't do small talk for the life of me, but it is a requirement as you head up to senior levels in corporations where networking is part of your role. Elegant dinners are still hell for me as I try to remember from the last one which side plate is mine and how to use layers of cutlery, as I've grown up eating with my hand or with only a fork. On many occasions I have eaten my dining companion's roll because I didn't know which was mine according to Western dining etiquette. Because I'm grown up now and understand context, I can laugh at my absence of Anglo-Saxon graces – but as a young black senior reporter and editor, these were mortifying things to deal with.

Yet, among my white colleagues, there was an ease and a comfort about navigating the corridors of power and building up a rapport with senior colleagues, which counted when decisions were made on who gets promoted and who does not.

If you are black and feel insecure or are quiet (or a fish out of water, like I often felt), incorrect conclusions can be drawn about your competence and abilities. The assets bequeathed by privilege are manifold and non-financial. It runs the gamut from having a driver's licence (and a car), being technologically savvy, having analytical skills (apartheid education stripped this from the syllabus in a deliberate act of malfeasance), a financial cushion to buffer one in the early years of work or entrepreneurship, regular holidays in the right places, and the appropriate school to give you the network asset.

The way competence and ability are measured is still an outcome of privilege and of the racialised networks that run (or used to run) the South African economy. It was an old boys' club and the numbers tell us the club has not sufficiently changed its rules.

Genuinely transformed, or altered, workplaces will compensate for asset deficiencies and enable young people to create new and different networks to see them on their way. There are wonderful examples where this has happened, but in the majority of experiences, it has not. There is a new cultural, social and political establishment that is black-led and which reflects the country, but the economic establishment is a work in still-too-early progress.

My colleague Muzi Kuzwayo, who writes for *City Press*, has been in the advertising and related industries for decades. He has studied and observed the pace of change in offices and boardrooms in South Africa. In a recent column, he wrote: 'Again, I am warning that white business in South Africa, because of resistance to change, is fertilising the ground for the rise of a black Adolf Hitler … Local business is no longer investing in South Africa, preferring to invest its money outside of our borders, citing BEE codes as the reason.'

───

The Johannesburg Stock Exchange. The site of listed wealth in South Africa. I find it one of the more transformed institutions, led as it is by two women: the chairperson Nonkululeko Nyembezi-Heita and the CEO Nicky Newton-King. If you look further down the organogram, the JSE has a number of women in senior roles and black men too.

It is no longer the forbidding place I used to believe it to be when it sat in an incongruous diamond-shaped building in Johannesburg's Diagonal Street. That must be because I put most of my savings into the JSE and so I've learnt how it works. I have unit trusts, retirement annuities and a pension fund all held by fund managers investing in companies listed on the JSE. It's my business to know how it works and which shares are doing what.

So, like many others, I am a shareholder and the outreach team at the JSE has done a lot to make me feel like one. You can play games to learn to trade or attend seminars or go online to get more information than you would be able to use in a lifetime. South Africa's JSE rates among the world's best for transparency, so information is easy enough to come by. It's an asset by any standard, and after its listing the share price has climbed steadily to display a place that is well run.

The JSE is also the populist politician's whipping boy. The young leader Julius Malema began his metamorphosis to political entrepreneur with a taste for Louis Vuitton and Breitling on the pavement outside the JSE. And it was a location he revisited to powerful effect in October 2015 as the leader of the EFF.

Back in 2011, Malema was building a profile as the ANC Youth League president. Traffic was at a standstill, though not a planned one like the Ecomobility World Festival I started writing about at the beginning of this chapter. That's lightweight street closure. It is political pandemonium when Malema, who is an ace political organiser, brings tens of thousands of unemployed youngsters to march on the JSE and then stages a long walk to freedom, which he plans to end at the Union Buildings, about 70 kilometres away in the political capital of Pretoria.

There is a festival atmosphere in Sandton as the young people take over the streets. They stage a sit-in outside the JSE where Malema rails against the fact that whites own capital and that's why young people are unemployed. It is a catchy sound bite and it helps to reinforce the perception of the JSE as the symbol of white wealth.

The gleaming granite towers over the youth marchers as Malema tests the campaign about economic freedom he will later use to start his own political party after he is thrown out of the governing ANC.

A few years later, President Jacob Zuma takes up the same narrative at a pre-election ANC meeting on economic trans-formation. Zuma has four or five different ministers in charge of economic policy. They all pull in different directions. At the same time, the Chinese economy slows down and the Tiger stops buying our commodities. The domestic and global economies combine to trap South Africa in a cruel phase of low growth that is almost entirely jobless.

There are between two million and three million increasingly impatient young people locked out of the job market. The presi-dent is under extreme pressure. In early 2015, he repeats the statistic in parliament: 'The black majority still owns only 3% of the Johannesburg Stock Exchange, pointing to the need to move faster to achieve meaningful economic emancipation.'

And thus he states that the reason black people are in a quan-dary is because they own only 3% of the JSE. President Zuma does not say it but he implies that whites, therefore, own 97% of wealth. Financial literacy in South Africa is not great (by late 2015, debt levels were at their worst since the start of the life of the National Credit Regulator) and so the shorthand version became that blacks owned 3% of all wealth while whites held 97%.

That's a good statistic to build a campaign on and it worked to ratchet up the pressure for an ANC win. It's also a completely incorrect statistic.

Exchange holdings are complex things. In fact, whites directly own 11% of the JSE, while blacks directly own 10%, according to an exhaustive research study commissioned by the JSE. Direct ownership by black people is measured as: BEE deals at listed level; BEE deals at subsidiary level; employee share ownership and other broad-based ownership schemes; and retail ownership (in the empowerment plans of MTN, Sasol, Naspers and the African Bank, among others).

On black ownership, the JSE says that government pension holders, largely blue-collar and middle-class workers, hold an additional 13% of the market. White people make up an added 11% of indirect ownership.

Who else owns our exchange? Foreigners, it turns out, hold the largest chunk, at about 39% at the end of 2013 – the foreign-held component has grown while individual and indirect holdings of black and white shareholders have stayed largely the same.

When Trevor Manuel became the finance minister, he tanked key indicators with the phrase 'amorphous markets' but the numbers here suggest he was right. We don't know enough about who owns what – a point reiterated in Piketty's Nelson Mandela Annual Lecture in October 2015.

While the country has adopted a system of broad-based empowerment in which ownership, skills development and procurement are all believed to be equally important to wealth transfer, the president's statement symbolises a new era. Only direct ownership by black tycoons now counts as empowerment, discounting the symbolism of what it means when so many more black people have assets invested on the JSE.

The National Empowerment Fund, a BEE investment and funding agency run by the state, supports the president's position and this has now set the benchmark – the agency does not correct the popular misperception that if 3% of the JSE is held by blacks, then 97% is held by whites. If this is how wealth is understood by high power, it is no surprise that money and who has it has become a combustible topic – but an inaccurate one.

One of the reasons that direct black ownership is low is because people sell and move on. Black direct ownership, for example, took a steep slide when Tokyo Sexwale unbundled his Mvelaphanda conglomerate. In other instances, the BEE lock-in period expires and people cash in their profit. Newton-King said indirect holdings by black people are a good thing as they evince savings and disposable income – happy economic indicators.

Investment writer Stuart Theobald, who runs the Intellidex consultancy, made an important observation about wealth ownership. He said what was being measured may be the problem because legal entities are difficult to assign a race to. 'We should focus on natural persons and only two things matter: what is their income, and what is their wealth. There is only one institution that knows the answers or at least tries to and that is the South African Revenue Service. If we want a proper tracking of transformation, that is where we should go for answers.'

I am a social democrat and so believe the pace of

indirect ownership of the JSE as well as the rate of black property ownership are far better indicators of well-being. Oligarchs
and princelings, the mega-beneficiaries of BEE, are neither here
nor there – they are important symbols and interesting to profile,
but I don't think the state's plan to create 100 black industrialists
will move the needle to take the figure of black indirect wealth
ownership nearer to the 40% mark that will represent a significantly changed proportion of wealth.

Not so, says Sandile Zungu, a delightful princeling who has
been at the forefront of black empowerment policy for well over
a decade. I ask him why we do not celebrate new wealth more
fulsomely and why the ANC does not claim this as its work,
which it is.

'Serious wealth has been created,' he says. 'BEE has worked.
We should acknowledge huge strides: the numbers of black
people who can travel overseas, who own farms, who drive posh
cars, who are contributing to big causes. Let's leverage on this
success and celebrate without saying, "Let them eat cake" (forgetting about the poor).'

He also dismisses the JSE's study of growing indirect ownership.
By including mandated investments (unit trusts, life policies and
retirement annuities), the JSE has delinked wealth creation from
control. In other words, black economic power is impotent if you
can't vote with it and can't determine the direction of companies.

'The issue of control must never be removed from the equation,' says Sandile.

———

Along with the barometer the JSE offers as insight into wealth distribution, there is the twin narrative that holds BEE to have been a largely unsuccessful enterprise: it is the one area where white and black elites concur but from radically different directions.

White conservatives tally up the numbers and pronounce that only a tiny proportion of black tycoons have benefited and that empowerment is largely a state-sponsored flop. Black business lobbyists right across the board will argue that BEE has hardly started properly and that white business is largely intransigent.

This set of perceptions is incorrect.

In 2015, Theobald reported that R317 billion worth of BEE deals had been done since 2001. He only measured the Top 100 companies, so it is probably higher. The *Financial Mail* reported: 'Of the R317 billion, R196 billion was attributable to strategic investment partners, R52 billion (16%) was attributable to employee schemes and R69 billion (22%) to broad-based community schemes.'

Benefits are real. Theobald quotes two examples: in FirstRand's R23.2-billion deal, the single biggest pay-off of R14.6 billion went to a broad-based trust. At Sanlam, more than half of the value of the R14.3-billion empowerment plan went to the insurer's partner, Patrice Motsepe.

Financial Mail writer Carol Paton poses the bigger question: is it enough? The tradable market value is R4.2 trillion, which places the value of BEE deals at a total of 7.5%.

It's not big enough. But here's another statistic to measure it against. The total value is double that spent on public housing stock since 1994. Housing is regarded as one of the good stories of political change in South Africa.

———

'Awakening on Friday morning, June 20, 1913, the South African Native found himself, not actually a slave, but a pariah in the land of his birth.' These were the words of journalist, politician and intellectual Sol Plaatje who toured the country by bicycle to see for himself the impact of the Natives Land Act, which came into force in 1913 and altered South Africa for good.

It stripped Africans of land and forbade them from ownership. It turned the majority into servants and serfs. Later on, the law was amended to increase African land ownership to 13% from 7% of the first law of displacement. This was a precursor to the homeland system and the barring of blacks from urban centres to peripheral group areas.

We are scarred, still, by the 1913 Natives Land Act. The three-page graphic that follows provides an overview of the history involved right up to the present-day situation. Between 1913 and 1989, 3.5 million black South Africans were forcibly driven off agricultural land and out of suburbs and towns – into far-flung reserves and racially designated locations. The cumulative effects on South African life and society were psychologically and physically profound and the damage is still being undone today.

If the JSE, as a measure of wealth, is unknown in large chunks, then so is land. Land, or land reform, this most emotive of post-apartheid issues, is hobbled by uncertainties.

———

1913

Black South Africans are decisively banned from the land. 'Awaking on Friday morning, June 20, 1913, the South African Native found himself, not actually a slave, but a pariah in the land of his birth.' These are the words of Sol T. Plaatje, the journalist, politician and intellectual who toured the country on a bicycle to see for himself the effects of the Land Act on black – and white – South Africans. His political masterwork, *Native Life in South Africa*, was published in 1916.

Land allocated to Africans by Natives Land Acts

The 1913 Natives Land Act barred all Africans from owning vast tracts of land in South Africa. The Act became law in June 1913, limiting African land ownership to 7%, though this would be increased to 13% later. Black people were restricted from buying or occupying land except as employees of a white master. It gave white people ownership of the rest of the land, leaving black people to scramble for the meagre leftovers. Widespread outrage – including white farmers who feared they could not carry on without their cheap and ready labour – had no effect on the legislators.

In his famous book, Plaatje explains the before-and-after scenario: 'A squatter in South Africa is a native who owns some livestock and, having no land of his own, hires a farm or grazing and ploughing rights from a landowner, to raise grain for his own use and feed his stock. Hence, these squatters are hit very hard by an Act which passed both houses of parliament during the session of 1913, received the signature of the Governor-General on June 16, was gazetted on June 19 and forthwith came into operation ...'

Plaatje describes the national impact as so great that most of those affected could not absorb the new reality. He writes: 'But the great revolutionary change thus wrought by a single stroke of the pen, in the condition of the native, was not realised by him until about the end of June. As a rule, many farm tenancies expire at the end of the half-year, so that in June 1913, not knowing that it was impracticable to make fresh contracts, some natives unwittingly went to search for new places of abode, which some farmers, ignorant of the law, quite as unwittingly accorded them. It was only when they went to register the new tenancies that the law officers of the Crown laid bare the cruel fact that to provide a landless native with accommodation was forbidden under a penalty of 100 pounds sterling, or six months' imprisonment. Then only was the situation realised.'

1937

The Natives Laws Amendment Act is passed, prohibiting the buying of land by Africans from whites in urban areas except by permission from government. Under the Act, authorities in urban areas keep a record of all Africans living in their jurisdictions.

1936

Building on the Natives Land Act, the 1936 Natives Trust and Land Act of South Africa comes into being. It suggests increasing African ownership to 13% from the 7% the Natives Land Act ruled in 1913.

1950

After winning the election in 1948, it takes the National Party only two years to start implementing even more drastic dispossession laws, including the Group Areas Act. This gives government power to create racially segregated areas defining where specific racial groups may live and work. The Act enables authorities to forcibly remove people from an area designated as belonging to another racial group. Prime Minister D.F. Malan appoints the Commission for the Socio-Economic Development of Bantu Areas, known as the Tomlinson commission, to develop a socio-economic plan to rehabilitate and develop black areas into 'self-governing' homelands.

How the land was lost Source: Graphics24.

1955

Sophiatown is declared a white area and more than 60 000 people are forcibly removed. A suburb gloatingly named Triomf is established in its place in 1957.

1953

The Tomlinson commission recommends separate development as a strategy to avoid racial tension in South Africa and urges an acceleration of land purchases to add to the homeland areas and address overcrowding.

1959

Lady Selbourne, north-west of Pretoria, was established in 1905 as an area where black people could own land. But the residents had been living under the threat of forced removals since the late 1940s, when government started threatening the township with evictions due to supposed overcrowding. African families are relocated to Ga-Rankuwa, Atteridgeville and Mamelodi. Indians are moved to Laudium and coloured people to Eersterust.

1966–67

District Six is declared a white area under the Group Areas Act and 60 000 people are forcibly removed to the Cape Flats, an area on the outer fringes of Cape Town. A year later, Simon's Town is declared a white area.

1969

About 3 000 Maluleke villagers are expelled from Pafuri, which is incorporated into the Kruger National Park. The Maluleke land claim will be one of the groundbreakers after 1994.

1968

At least 2 500 members of the Bakwena Ba Mogopa are forcibly relocated from their farm, Swartrand, in an area that would become the North West province, to Ledig near Sun City. The community had bought their farm just before the 1913 Natives Land Act was passed, but government does not like the farm sitting at the heart of white-owned farmland. Evictions continue into the 1980s.

1976

The president issues an order for the removal of 400 families from a number of small reserves near Humansdorp in the lower Tsitsikamma forest to Elukhanyweni in Ciskei. Police are ordered to arrest those who refuse to move.

1977

The squatter camps of Unibel and Modderdam on the outskirts of Cape Town are demolished without a court order.

1982

In a watershed court judgment in favour of a Mrs Govendor [*sic*], Justice Richard Goldstone rules that the Group Areas Act does not empower government to automatically evict a person. Government, he rules, is obliged to provide alternative accommodation.

1991

On 1 February, President F.W. de Klerk revokes the 1913 and 1936 land acts through the enactment of the Abolition of Racially Based Land Measures Act and the Upgrading of Land Tenure Act. Negotiations begin on how to restore land in a new South Africa.

1989

The Bakwena Ba Mogopa people win their court challenge. Their eviction from Swartrand is declared unlawful and they are given the right to reoccupy the land.

1983

At least 20 000 donkeys belonging to local black farmers are killed by the Bophuthatswana government in what becomes known as the Bophuthatswana Donkey Massacre. Government justifies its actions by arguing that cattle are more deserving of grass than donkeys.

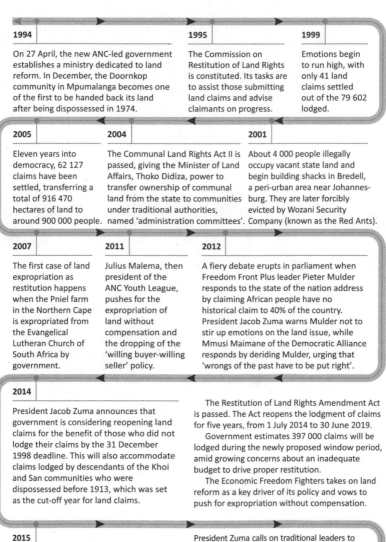

1994

On 27 April, the new ANC-led government establishes a ministry dedicated to land reform. In December, the Doornkop community in Mpumalanga becomes one of the first to be handed back its land after being dispossessed in 1974.

1995

The Commission on Restitution of Land Rights is constituted. Its tasks are to assist those submitting land claims and advise claimants on progress.

1999

Emotions begin to run high, with only 41 land claims settled out of the 79 602 lodged.

2005

Eleven years into democracy, 62 127 claims have been settled, transferring a total of 916 470 hectares of land to around 900 000 people.

2004

The Communal Land Rights Act II is passed, giving the Minister of Land Affairs, Thoko Didiza, power to transfer ownership of communal land from the state to communities under traditional authorities, named 'administration committees'.

2001

About 4 000 people illegally occupy vacant state land and begin building shacks in Bredell, a peri-urban area near Johannesburg. They are later forcibly evicted by Wozani Security Company (known as the Red Ants).

2007

The first case of land expropriation as restitution happens when the Pniel farm in the Northern Cape is expropriated from the Evangelical Lutheran Church of South Africa by government.

2011

Julius Malema, then president of the ANC Youth League, pushes for the expropriation of land without compensation and the dropping of the 'willing buyer-willing seller' policy.

2012

A fiery debate erupts in parliament when Freedom Front Plus leader Pieter Mulder responds to the state of the nation address by claiming African people have no historical claim to 40% of the country. President Jacob Zuma warns Mulder not to stir up emotions on the land issue, while Mmusi Maimane of the Democratic Alliance responds by deriding Mulder, urging that 'wrongs of the past have to be put right'.

2014

President Jacob Zuma announces that government is considering reopening land claims for the benefit of those who did not lodge their claims by the 31 December 1998 deadline. This will also accommodate claims lodged by descendants of the Khoi and San communities who were dispossessed before 1913, which was set as the cut-off year for land claims.

The Restitution of Land Rights Amendment Act is passed. The Act reopens the lodgment of claims for five years, from 1 July 2014 to 30 June 2019.

Government estimates 397 000 claims will be lodged during the newly proposed window period, amid growing concerns about an inadequate budget to drive proper restitution.

The Economic Freedom Fighters takes on land reform as a key driver of its policy and vows to push for expropriation without compensation.

2015

Government says nearly 60 000 'claims as lodged' have been finalised, benefiting about 368 000 households and 1.8 million individuals. R7.6 billion in financial compensation has been paid out and a total of 3 million hectares awarded, at a total cost of R15.4 billion.

Speaking at the opening of the National House of Traditional Leaders in Cape Town,

President Zuma calls on traditional leaders to put together a team of 'good lawyers' to take advantage of the Restitution of Land Rights Amendment Bill.

In his state of the nation address, the president says the Regulation of Land Holdings Bill will be submitted to parliament this year, limiting land ownership by foreigners.

He indicates that a new Expropriation Act will also be enacted this year.

In 2013, the chief surveyor-general Mmuso Riba said figures on race and nationality in ownership of land were unavailable. 'One of the things we wanted to achieve out of this exercise was to determine race classification in terms of ownership of land in

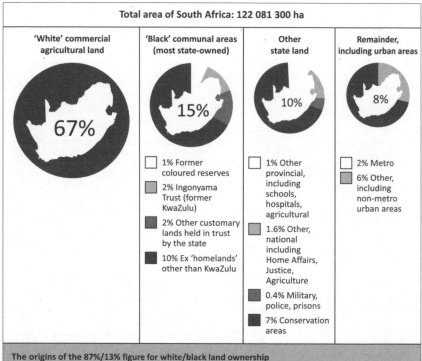

Total area of South Africa: 122 081 300 ha

'White' commercial agricultural land	'Black' communal areas (most state-owned)	Other state land	Remainder, including urban areas
67%	15%	10%	8%

'Black' communal areas (most state-owned)
- 1% Former coloured reserves
- 2% Ingonyama Trust (former KwaZulu)
- 2% Other customary lands held in trust by the state
- 10% Ex 'homelands' other than KwaZulu

Other state land
- 1% Other provincial, including schools, hospitals, agricultural
- 1.6% Other, national including Home Affairs, Justice, Agriculture
- 0.4% Military, police, prisons
- 7% Conservation areas

Remainder, including urban areas
- 2% Metro
- 6% Other, including non-metro urban areas

The origins of the 87%/13% figure for white/black land ownership

The 87:13 ratio of white to black ownership of land derives from an apartheid blueprint based on the Land Acts of 1913 and 1936 that had not been completely implemented by 1994. Under apartheid, South Africa was divided between a core of about 85% of the country deemed 'white' politically, and a periphery of 10 ethnically defined 'African' 'homelands', plus a number of tiny 'coloured' reserves. Race-based land possession and relocation caused suffering and hardship for millions of black South Africans (SPP 1983) but failed to realise the master plan. Throughout the twentieth century growing numbers of 'Africans' and most 'coloureds' continued to live in so-called white South Africa, with varying levels of tenure security on white-owned farms and conservation lands, in urban areas, and even on a small number of black-owned properties that escaped forced removals.

'The land should be owned by all who live on it' – Freedom Charter

Source: Institue for Poverty, Land and Agrarian Studies (PLAAS), University of the Western Cape.

South Africa. Unfortunately we could not do that because the Home Affairs database is no longer classified (by) race.' By the time *City Press* checked again in 2015, the position remained the same.

The best figures available are from the land activist organisation, PLAAS, which drew on the land audit to make the following finding: 67% of South Africa's land is held by white commercial interests, with 15% held in black communal areas by traditional and communal property authorities. The state owns 10% in direct holdings while 8% of our land is in coveted urban areas.

So, where are we? By the 1998 cut-off for the first phase of land restitution and reform claims, 79 602 claims were lodged.

In 2015, President Zuma said 60 000 claims, as lodged, had been finalised, benefiting about 368 000 households and 1.8 million individuals. An amount of R7.6 billion in financial compensation had been paid out and a total of three million hectares awarded, at a cost of R15.4 billion.

Government has reopened the land claims process to take account of dispossession that occurred before 1913 and to allow further claimants to stake their rights.

By May 2015, more than 55 000 land claims had been lodged in all nine provinces, as the diagram detailing these new land claims by province, on the following page, shows.

Because land reform and restitution have moved at a snail's pace, politicians will often argue that the apartheid inheritance of whites owning 87% of the land and blacks owning 13% has not shifted. The reason for the slow pace and the reality of ownership is deeply complicated, with important work being done to

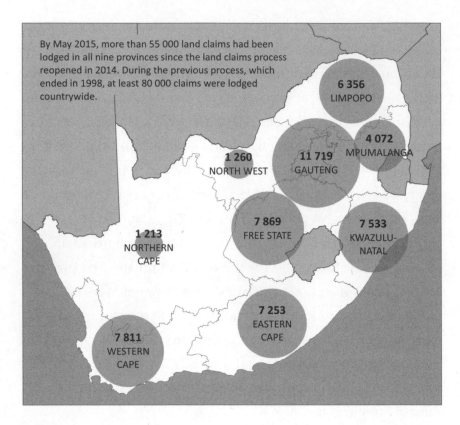

By May 2015, more than 55 000 land claims had been lodged in all nine provinces since the land claims process reopened in 2014. During the previous process, which ended in 1998, at least 80 000 claims were lodged countrywide.

6 356
LIMPOPO

4 072
MPUMALANGA

1 260
NORTH WEST

11 719
GAUTENG

1 213
NORTHERN
CAPE

7 869
FREE STATE

7 533
KWAZULU-
NATAL

7 253
EASTERN
CAPE

7 811
WESTERN
CAPE

South Africa's new land claims

Source: Graphics24.

show that without agricultural extension support, vast tracts of restored or reformed land lie fallow. There are, of course, notable exceptions, but on the whole, the pattern of people's movement is an exodus out of the country into the towns and cities.

Another regular red herring populists use is to employ the fear of foreigners buying up vast tracts of land and displacing black hopes and aspirations. But South Africa's government does not currently know exactly how much land is foreign-owned.

There are some preliminary figures available from an August 2007 study, conducted by a panel of experts and presented to the then minister of agriculture and land affairs, Lulu Xingwana. According to this presentation: 'As far as ownership by foreign corporations and trusts is concerned, statistics are incomplete and extremely difficult to collect and interpret ...

'The Panel concluded that foreign natural persons own 3% (and a significantly higher percentage in coastal and game farming areas) of land in the categories of erwen (land used for residential housing), agricultural holdings, farm land and sectional titles.

'The size and value of foreign ownership will certainly be higher once the process of analyzing information regarding corporations, trusts and Section 21 companies is completed.'

According to the state land audit carried out by the office of South Africa's surveyor-general in 2013: 'In terms of land use, most of South Africa is under natural pasture (73.2%), approximately 12% is arable productive land, and about the same proportion is allocated to nature conservation while only about 1% of the land is currently used for urban and residential purposes.'

In urban land ownership, the picture is far better. Black people (including coloureds and Indians) make up almost half of all house purchases, with black Africans accounting for 30%, according to First National Bank's Estate Agent Survey of early 2015.

The survey stated: 'While the racial transformation of residential property buying has come a long way, the survey has also pointed to a lack of further progress since 2008, which arguably speaks to mediocre economic performance since the end of the boom years around that year.'

The South African Institute of Race Relations includes these details on urban property. 'Out of 11 594 000 African homes, 6 622 000, or 57%, are owned and fully paid off.' Of these, 2.3 million were Reconstruction and Development Programme (RDP) houses and a further 400 000 were old township stock transferred to families who lived in them.

Because my family had moved home so often from one rental to the next as I grew up and my enterprising mother tried to keep us out of Group Areas clutches, I bought a property with indecent haste as soon as I could. Roots were such elusive things that I tried to plant them as soon as possible. Property has been a revelation to me – I've never lost money as I traded up from flat to townhouse to free-standing home and used the collateral in ways I could not have imagined when I made my first purchase.

———

Wealth redistribution and creation are not at ground zero.

In an article for *City Press*, Naspers chairperson Koos Bekker wrote: '[I]magine all the income generated in South Africa today (from cash, shares, property, factories, etc.) as a round apple. Now cut away that part that existed at the moment of transition in 1994. What do you find? Only slightly more than half of our total wealth today (55%) existed in former president F.W. de

Klerk's last year – almost half (45%) was generated under ANC governance: new wealth, created after apartheid.'

But the opinion shapers regularly put out the message that nothing has changed. Although black progress under a black government has been significant on all levels, thought leaders with access to mass media hardly ever reflect this with good intention. The net effect is a country that does not pat itself on the back often enough for what has been achieved.

Take one of our finest political analysts, S'Thembiso Msomi, writing in the *Sunday Times* as the xenophobic flames horrified a strand of South Africans who understand our destiny as inextricably linked to the continent we call home. Msomi said the education system had not sufficiently Africanised teaching syllabuses. Then he added this: '[L]ink that with the entrenchment of a largely racially based socio-economic order that has whites at the top, Indians and coloureds in the middle and the black poor at the bottom – then you have trouble.'

Of course, South African inequality is a recipe for disaster, but the social pyramid does not look like it used to under apartheid. We need to turn the pyramid on its head, not see the holy grail as getting blacks to the position of a white elite. In my opinion, that's the wrong goal, but it is easier to understand South Africa in its old binaries rather than grapple with its new complexities.

In a *Sowetan* opinion article ahead of the commemoration of Black Wednesday on 19 October, Nelvis Qekema writes about why nothing has substantively changed since the banning of Black Consciousness organisations, individuals and newspapers on that awful day in 1977. 'What sometimes makes people take the foot off the pedal of the Struggle is their inability to differentiate between the governing party, the ANC, and the ruling class – white minority capital.'

This meme is common – that the governing ANC is a cipher, while the ruling class remains white.

The ANC does not rule over the shell of a state that is funded by foreign donors: the state is by any measure (tax, regulation, its substantial procurement budget, its employees) *the* most powerful player in the economy and polity. It is the ruling class – although I prefer to call it the governing class or the government.

Thami Mazwai, one of the fathers of South African journalism, and now a specialist in entrepreneurship, writes a column in *Business Day*. At about the same time as Msomi's column, Mazwai wrote one entitled 'Status quo has not changed since 1994', in which he argued: 'The reality is that white SA has not risen to the challenge of making up for the sins of the past. While some businesses have initiatives to better the lives of their black staff and black people in general, many fight tooth and nail to retain the privileges apartheid bestowed on them.'

That may well be so, but the numbers don't tell the same story – there has been significant black agency and black progress. This is insufficient for the challenges of our time, but the answer is not to 'go back to the drawing board' – an opinion I read and hear every week – but rather to work out how to move to a second phase of development now.

The psychological leap between thinking we are at ground zero and giving ourselves a pat on the back is huge but necessary.

Rather than beating ourselves up, we should be saying 'well

done'. What's next requires an act of national self-confidence and a reconditioning of how we understand our first score of democracy and freedom.

———

As a newspaper editor, I get to do a lot of public speaking by way of guest lectures and panel contributions. My topics are usually about current affairs, politics and the state of the nation. A few years ago, I decided to do these talks, make these contributions, in perfect halves to illustrate something about South Africa: there is great and not so great; big challenges, big achievements; more light than dark.

There are few developing countries and almost none on our continent that have extended a social welfare net to a good third of its citizens as we do. It is a significant achievement and a symbol of human solidarity. There is more, lots more. The electrification programme has been so good that it has now put the grid under significant pressure. The extension of piped water has changed lives. Making health care free for pregnant women and children has significantly dropped the rate of maternal mortality.

South Africa has achieved a democratic dividend. It's not enough, but neither is it nothing.

Take Sandton. The group of us who do the walk from Sandton to Alex at the beginning of Transport Month are quite a mix but largely black.

The cutest person there is a little girl, possibly about four years old, who rides her pink Barbie tricycle. Her dad is on a mountain bike and he looks buff.

About halfway there, the cutie decides she's had enough, so she trudges to the shade and her dad pushes one bike and carries the other.

We all ride back to Sandton in Metro buses. Most of the people who are in the bus are obviously middle class (bikes, skateboards, fancy takkies tell the story) and not resident in Alex.

Wazimap.co.za, an excellent data site, shows that Alex is 99% black by census result. Neighbouring wards in Sandton are an average 30% black African and about half white if you add in coloured and Indian people. That is quite a change in two decades or so since the Group Areas Act was scrapped.

So, back to Alex. Alex gave me the first taste of fear in my mouth when I covered the violence between Inkatha-aligned members who lived in the hostels and the comrades of the surrounding township. It was bloody in the early 1990s and the air was dead with the hopelessness of violence.

Slowly, the message of peace filtered in from Kempton Park where negotiators spent years hammering out a transfer of power. Inkatha leader Mangosuthu Buthelezi was brought into the fold of peace and Alex stopped being a no-go zone. For years, I covered the Alexandra Renewal Programme and watched as billions of rands were poured in. You can see the impacts today.

But another salutary lesson for understanding South Africa in the twenty-first century is also there to observe: we do not spend money well, and bureaucracy and infighting can impede development. With the billions of rands poured into Alexandra, it should work better.

In Alex, Emmanuel Sithole's killers tell a story of those left behind. All the young men who were party to his death have hard-working, world-weary mothers who tried their best to claw their boys from the life of gangsterism and crime it is still too easy to sink into. A few live in the hostels, which are supposed to have long been altered into family accommodation.

The fit among the three levels of government – national, provincial and local – has not been seamless enough to develop this old community in significant enough ways. Public transport links have not been adequately planned or implemented (though there are promises that this will change) and public security is still too often a halcyon dream.

As is true for South Africa as a whole, a working Alexandra depends on a state that functions better. This is often the elephant in the room of our race debate – state function or dysfunction and the extent to which this is or is not responsible for a better freedom.

6

#REVOLUTION

I had become that person. Self-satisfied and middle class. Every time I read an article about whiteness, the school of thought that believes the world is constructed to support and maintain white power and capitalism, I sighed and turned the page.

Once on a panel on the topic, I was impatient and rude. When I heard interesting young people define their understanding of contemporary South Africa as one still governed by white supremacy, there was more than once I exclaimed, in exasperation, 'Oh, come on, you're joking.' I still do not find it a persuasive philosophy, but I do now understand its popularity.

Deeply proud of our founding story, I am an unapologetic disciple of the founding president and statesman President Nelson Mandela and his sidekick priest and fellow Nobel Peace Prize winner, Archbishop Emeritus Desmond Tutu. Their philosophies of peace and Ubuntu resonate in my soul; I like their bravery and take-no-prisoners style. I like how they moulded us from the smelter of apartheid into a rainbow nation under the African sun. It is almost an anathema to so declare your discipleship these days, but there it is.

But I had also become part of the establishment and, for a journalist, I had lost my sense of curiosity about what made a generation see so differently from the way I did through my precious rose-coloured spectacles. I still wear those spectacles, but this book has been my effort to see through my own myopia.

Why weren't more people grateful for their freedom and taking it and running for dear life like a pursued Bok with a rugby ball on an English field? Like I had.

This book has been my listening journey to bring me to a deeper understanding of where we are. Listening, thinking and contemplating had become arts I practised less often than I should have as the pace of the news world had turned me towards efficiency and solution-seeking. 'Let's just get on with it,' seemed to be my failsafe position. 'Let's make this country.'

For many reasons, I am a big fan of former Finance Minister Trevor Manuel, but mostly because the National Development Plan that he drew up with a commission of the great and the good is a perfect blueprint of how to grow and make prosperous this beautiful country. So, instead of spending time picking at the sores of the past, I was yelling at my compatriots, 'Let's just implement The Plan.' And then it will all be fine.

Except it won't. We are not there. The work is not done. Our country is not ready to move into the future at the pace of Singapore or Rwanda or to toss the past into the past in ways that I've witnessed in Vietnam and a few other post-conflict countries that have gone on a high-growth and directed political path. Our reckoning is not done and that reckoning increasingly takes a racial tone. It is what it is and it is where we are. The idea of a deeper and more resonant social justice and racial justice is taking hold in South Africa, with a majority opinion turning against the idea that we are a rainbow nation under God as Tutu first christened us. Maybe one day, but not this day.

The Student Spring of 2015 drives this home most clearly. Other than in the business community, the students who brought their campuses and the country to a standstill for a week brought a message that echoed: there is lots more work to be done, and we can start with what have become increasingly impossible to pay: university fees. In this most profound of times for me, I now know the reckoning is nowhere near done. The unfinished business of colonialism and apartheid will be finished by a new generation.

The story of contemporary global progress is under-told – as is the story of South African progress. The idea of the Millennium Development Goals galvanised good people. Maternal mortality is going down. So is hunger. There are more children in school in poor countries than ever before. Aids, TB and other communicable diseases are on the way to becoming eradicable. This is good news.

But there is another side. Pumping fortunes are being made but these are increasingly going to the moneyed, as economist Thomas Piketty has argued in his seminal *Capital in the Twenty-First Century*. This has created a massive and yawning wealth gap with the 1% (the title given to the super-wealthy) often owning more than the entire GDP of poorer developing countries.

In South Africa, the pattern is the same: new fortunes are being made and being replicated, but around the globe and here, the left-behind are too large. The South African under-class is too big. The middle class is too small. And the dominant class in

business is too white and too far removed from the real South
Africa.

———

As I complete this book, my publisher is getting anxious, but I
can't press the stop button. In the end, the final chapter writes
itself as October unfolds into a mini-revolution.

Gaga about spring, I have a wardrobe full of purple and pink
clothes – the colours of the blooms I love best. This year, I am
high on jacarandas – in Pretoria and Johannesburg in South
Africa and in Nairobi and Naivasha in Kenya. These beautiful
invasive aliens are being neutered because they gulp our diminishing water resources, but they still represent the thaw of winter,
warmth and good times to me.

So, we've been to see the white jacarandas in Pretoria. And
gone to the Union Buildings (two days after students marched
on it) to take images of the purple flowers against a gunmetal
grey sky. Mandela loved them, too, and at the Union Buildings
his beatific statue beams down – although I could swear I saw
his statue grimace when the lawns became a battle zone late in
October 2015.

In Johannesburg, the trees grow in entire avenues covering
the north of the city in a purple haze. At this time of the year, my
alma mater, Wits, is strewn in petals that mark the point before
exams when you should have started studying or else you are in
deep shit. As I write in the middle of the protests, the incoming

SRC president, Nompendulo Mkhatshwa (with Shaeera Kalla, the outgoing SRC president), had become the face of the student uprising. She is reflected in powerful images leading marches over the strewn petals.

During this spring in 2015, the flowers are also the students. The image of this most amazing 10 days in October is the aerial shot – of students filling Plein Street outside parliament; then the street outside Luthuli House at the governing ANC's headquarters; and then the lawns at the Union Buildings. In the images, the T-shirts of red, yellow and some blue are like spring blooms renewing a path, redefining freedom and struggle and helping South Africa find itself.

It starts with the #RhodesMustFall movement at UCT in March 2015. On 21 March, the first #FeesMustFall is tweeted by @SkhumbuzoTuswa. Then in October, it is like watching a field of promise come into bloom as it spreads from campus to campus. *City Press* counts the movement as it spreads by social media across 17 campuses in 10 days.

UCT succeeds in interdicting students who are disrupting movement into and out of the campus as well as stopping staff and students who want to continue classes. #RhodesMustFall and #FeesMustFall are cited as respondents – a step-change in student politics and a signifier of how social media and social movements will drive protest. If you look carefully at the movements, there are no clear leaders – increasingly it is a collective with crowds, which grow almost organically.

Wits is shuttered for days and it is clear the university council is hither and thither, not knowing which way to move.

The universities are exploding one by one. When it started at UCT in March, #RhodesMustFall went from a meme to a front-page and top-of-bulletin story that gripped the imagination of the country.

That this is a hashtag-spread revolt tells a story and assumes an asset – a smartphone. The mass of students arraigned in this amazing protest tells another story: access. In 21 years, the democratic state has substantially scaled access to universities. This was a journey that apartheid's crazed demagogues had specially ensured they should never make.

So, the protest is a story of freedom, too. And, by and large, the students who make it into university are middle class or have parents who want them to become so, in order to pull up those left behind. In countless student testimonies, the young people revealed the responsibilities on their shoulders: to lift up a brother and sister; to pay for a gran's first home; to support a struggling parent who had scraped to send them to campus.

Listen. The students spoke in the timbre of privilege. What was their weapon at parliament when the cops used apartheid tactics? Bottled water. They wore hip clothes. And had access to resources: lawyers, buses, counsellors and cars. They were not the under-class of youth.

They were, it seemed to me, freedom's children. Here's the rub I learnt: when you bring black children onto formerly white campuses, the generational privilege of their white compatriots is a cruel thing to countenance because you realise the extent of your disenfranchisement even 21 years into freedom. And, as your white compatriots plan gap years, take luxurious holidays and have money to burn, what is your lot?

You've got to make it out of campus and into work double-quick to pay off that loan and begin to make good on being The Graduate. Holidays are a foreign concept – and when the campus tries to kick you out of residence during holidays to rent out the hostels to holidaymakers, this drives resentment and resistance (as it has at Rhodes). You have no spending money and the world of plenty you've been thrust into (the city centres where the protests have been biggest) is as impenetrable and unaffordable as if you were looking through glass.

Wits student leader Mcebo Dlamini said at Luthuli House: we also want to be able to eat at Rosebank. Many students told horror survival stories of prostituting themselves, becoming the girlfriends of sugar daddies, keeping up three jobs to afford fees. And where your white compatriot (and the odd black one) might look forward to an inherited endowment and other assets (such as a car) to see them on their way, for many black students, you end university with a debt sentence.

#FeesMustFall is about much more than fees – it is about freedom's unfinished work and its soldiers are the children of that freedom; it is also about choices the democratic state has made. The so-called born-frees – born just before or after 1994.

At the beginning of this movement, I am on the wrong foot. I had thought, a statue? Aren't there bigger things to worry about? (Like getting your degree and getting on with building our country and implementing The Plan.)

The statue of Cecil John Rhodes, and of others, later in the

Student Spring of 2015, have become symbols of an incomplete transition – curriculums that still hold Europe and the West as the fulcrums around which they turn; too-high fees; too-large a gap between management and workers. And in the student uprising, a statue becomes a site of a racial conflagration. At North-West University, white students surround the statue of Totius – the Afrikaner poet who first translated the Bible – while black students try to tear it down from its plinth as they saw their comrades successfully achieve at UCT in April.

While the first generation of freedom fighters imbued by the spirit of reconciliation had left university building names largely unchanged, the new generation decided a rose by any other name did not smell as sweet. Renaming buildings and removing statues are key to cultural transformation now; our founding fathers had retained names as part of the first transition to freedom.

A building at uber-Afrikaans Stellenbosch University is renamed Winnie Mandela House; the Bremner Building at UCT is now unofficially Azania House. The administrative block at Wits, called Senate House, is renamed Solomon House after the Umkhonto we Sizwe martyr Solomon Mahlangu who died at 23 years of age. A haunting song called 'Solomon' becomes the anthem of the fee revolt.

If you drill down into the protests and look at its armoury of tweets and posters, there is more going on – it is a challenge to the fundament of the South African transition from the market economy (which includes fee-paying universities and the out-sourcing of the blue-collar workforce) to the idea of a rainbow nation and the overhaul of curriculums. This will be a significant narrative theme of South African public life in 2016 as the ideas underpinning #RhodesMustFall quickly leapfrog into politics, with radical policies quickly shaped on land, the media and the economy. Our politics will be radicalised by a new generation.

University should be free. Student after student quotes the Freedom Charter: 'The Doors of Learning and Culture shall be opened', and, later in the protest, successive ANC resolutions to make tertiary education free are dragged out from the archive and paraded on social media and in the many marches that students hold across the country.

The establishment is regarded as opposition territory – the mass media are thrown out of meetings and new incumbents allowed privileged access. This reminds me of how, during apartheid's dying days, I had access as a *Weekly Mail* reporter that others from the then established order did not. What a turnabout!

History repeats itself like the times in the sixties, seventies and eighties when student movements prodded the country in directions it needed to go.

The uber-powerful secretary general of the ANC, Gwede Mantashe, comes down to meet the students who march from their Braamfontein and Auckland Park campuses to the downtown head office of Africa's oldest liberation movement.

The party's laid on a stage, which the students eschew. They make him wait as they go through their programme and then decide he must sit among them as their vice-chancellor Adam Habib had been made to do six days before. After Habib, all vice-chancellors lose the stature of office and are brought down to be with the people. At UCT, the acting vice-chancellor and his peers are also made to sit among students on the hot tarmac. At other campuses, there is no vested authority as it is overturned and students set the programme and the pace. The week sees a succession of vice-chancellors communicating on the ground and through student-owned megaphones.

The idea of making powerful individuals be part of the people in an era of the VIP-isation of society is catchy. At parliament, the South African Communist Party leader and Minister of Higher Education and Training Blade Nzimande is called outside. The megaphone gives up the ghost and so does he, retreating to the comfort of a knowable power.

Mantashe grumbles: there is a difference between humbling yourself and being humiliated. He is not given a platform to speak but must take the memorandum back upstairs to Luthuli House with him. *Amandla!* Where does it lie? It has certainly shifted. As ANC leaders receive students through the week, they are like a stereotype come alive. Fattened by power, nearly all have the *mqaba* of power – the pot belly that tells of a good life. They wear suits or dark jackets – another symbol of office. To me, they look lost and bewildered, unsure of what to do with a mass movement they neither created nor understand.

The party allows a retreat into militarisation – in the National Assembly, MPs who asked proceedings to stop to take account of the students outside are bundled out by white-shirted elite police officers recently hired for their bulk. Minister of State Security David Mahlobo takes a central role at parliament, Luthuli House and again at the Union Buildings – signalling that the student protest is not seen as a social justice one but as a threat to the state.

165

Students are tear-gassed, arrested and beaten – they are toughed. Then the party attempts to change its mind. The preparation of the stage to welcome students suggests so. From there, it tries to own this struggle, highlighting its policy resolutions on free tertiary education. The genie is out of the bottle and the shift feels tectonic.

In the end, the students resolve beautifully my question about whites and where we are and where we are headed. The campus is the crucible of the land.

Government and political authority have changed – the private sector much less so. I am enormously influenced by Deputy Chief Justice Dikgang Moseneke's view that in the professions and in business, the dominant class is white and that the power of the sector suggests the entirety of society is under-transformed. This has expanded my understanding of dominance and governance.

Unlike the eighties, the phase of student protest I know best, this time whites were not centred during the Student Spring in 2015 – but they were part of the protests in solidarity and, in some cases, for matching needs. In other words, they were equals. The resources of privileged students (largely but not all white) were leveraged in the form of lawyers, lifts and other resources. It struck me as how it should be, and a lesson for those parts of South African society where deep structural transformation has not shifted sufficiently.

In a country built on the principles of equality, representivity and justice, it is pretty clear to me that representation is important – as the next brewing race fight in the legal profession will reveal to us further down. The boardrooms and nearly all economic sectors have much work to do.

The stories of two white students show how a new generation may understand its role differently to that of a dominant or special class that often accompanies writing or thinking about whites as a group.

In a post, Markus Trengove, one of the students arrested at UCT, wrote: 'I benefited from the injustice of apartheid. Although I did not choose it, my race, gender and language have allowed me to inherit certain privileges. The right response is no longer to bury my head in shame. The right response is not try and guard these privileges. The right reaction is to admit that there is an enormous injustice, but that my privilege has put me in a good position to remedy it. That is my privilege. That is my duty.'

Jacques Swart, a Tshwane University of Technology student, attends the protest at the Union Buildings wearing a Boks T-shirt (it is the day before the semi-final against the All Blacks) and he tells *City Press*: 'I went to the Union Buildings, danced, sang and even threw a rock – and it was all worth it. I will continue to be part of the struggle to achieve free education. There must be a way.'

Swart joins the movement out of identification with the struggle against fees. His mum is struggling and she tells *City Press* that if she didn't work in Hartebeespoort, she would have joined the protest. She is putting three children through university at a cost of R200 000 a year and she is buckling.

I don't want to over-analyse, but it seemed from watching the role of white students that something very good had happened.

UNIVERSITY OF THE WITWATERSRAND

The @WitsPYA account first tweets #WitsFeesMustFall on 8 Oct in response to a 10.5% fee increase. The vice-chancellor, Adam Habib, and members of his council meet with students on Fri, 16 Oct. Senate House occupied and renamed Solomon Mahlangu House. Medical campus occupied. Lectures and exams cancelled on Tues, 20 Oct. Students, with UJ students, organise huge march to Luthuli House on Thurs, 22 Oct.

UNIVERSITY OF JOHANNESBURG

#UJShutDown first appears on 20 July, tweeted by @EFF_UJ_Soweto. It appears again on 21 Oct, a day ahead of UJ joining the protests. #UJFeesMustFall first tweeted on 14 Oct by @Killa_assessino. UJ students protest at their Auckland Park and Soweto campuses on Thurs, 22 Oct, and march to Luthuli House with Wits students. Violence erupts on their return, clashes with private security. Damage to property.

TSHWANE UNIVERSITY OF TECHNOLOGY

#TUTFeesMustFall first tweeted on 14 Oct by @Uncle_JayB. Campus rocked by protests and burning tyres. Students have a tradition of protest at TUT. On Wed, 21 Oct, students barricade entrance to university, blocking cars. TUT students accused of intimidating protesters at the Union Building march on Fri, 23 Oct. #Sunnyside7 arrested after Union Buildings march.

*No tweet data available for the Tshwane University of Technology

UNIVERSITY OF PRETORIA

#TuksFeesMustFall is first tweeted as early as 29 Sept by @Miss_Shumba calling students to a protest. On Fri, 23 Oct, the #UPRising movement is central to the march on the Union Buildings. Protests begin on Wed, 21 Oct, after the vice-chancellor, Cheryl de la Rey, fails to satisfy students at a meeting. They occupy the amphitheatre and student centre and take to the streets, shutting down campus.

TRENDING PEAK

#FeesMustFall and #NationalShutDown trended worldwide, reaching a peak on 21–22 Oct 2015

200 000 tweets
#FeesMustFall

100 000 tweets
#NationalShutDown

KEY

Total tweets contributed by each university in the 30 days up to 24 Oct 2015.
Source: ROi Africa
First tweet data via ctrlq.org

NWU **4.3%**

LIMPOPO

University of Limpopo **1.38%**

Unisa **1.09%**
GAUTENG

NORTH WEST

Tuks **4.14%**
UJ **8.69%**
Wits **18.95%**
FREE STATE

MPUMALANGA

KWAZULU-NATAL

NORTHERN CAPE

EASTERN CAPE

WESTERN CAPE

*No tweet data available for the University of Venda

@SkhumbuzoTuswa first used the phrase #FeesMustFall on Twitter on 21 March 2015. His tweet was a reflection on UCT's #RhodesMustFall movement that would pull down the statue of Cecil John Rhodes on campus in April 2015 in a campaign to decolonise universities.

NORTH-WEST UNIVERSITY, POTCHEFSTROOM

#NWUFeesMustFall first tweeted on 18 Oct by @MO_kAtz7. Reform PUK movement launches on mostly white campus on Thurs, 13 Oct. Statue of Afrikaans poet Totius becomes site of contention between black and white students. After unsuccessful engagement with management, first protest held on Fri, 23 Oct, outside campus. Gates locked on students.

NORTH-WEST UNIVERSITY, MAFIKENG

#NWUMafikeng in the context of #FeesMustFall first appears on 21 Oct in a tweet from @ConverseChatty1. The Mafikeng campus is closed on the same day following protests and incidents of damage to property. In a huge police swoop, some 41 students are arrested for public violence.

UNIVERSITY OF MPUMALANGA

Though there is no official hashtag, the 300 students studying at the campus shut it down and later join forces with Sol Plaatje University to take to the streets of Nelspruit on Thurs, 22 Oct. The university, established in 2014, is forced to suspend construction and classes.

UNIVERSITY OF VENDA

#UNIVENFeesMustFall is first tweeted on 19 Oct by @Witnessed87. Two weeks before, EFF spokesperson Fana Mokoena posts pictures of cockroaches and crumbling facilities at Univen on Twitter, causing outrage. On Fri, 23 Oct, thousands of students are led in protest by their first female SRC president, Mashudo Julian.

How Twitter helped to fuel and maintain the student uprising
Source: Graphics24.

UNIVERSITY OF THE WESTERN CAPE
#UWCFeesMustFall first tweeted on 16 Oct by @tauffeq. #UWCShutDown first tweeted on 20 Oct. UWC students part of the parliament march on Wed, 21 Oct. Police use stun grenades, water cannons and rubber bullets on students on Thurs, 22 Oct, and in a dramatic off-campus march on Fri, 23 Oct. Students granted a high court interdict preventing police from using excessive force.

UNIVERSITY OF THE FREE STATE
#UFSFeesMustFall first tweeted by @Uncle_JayB on 14 Oct. Campus is closed on Wed, 21 Oct, when protests break out on all three campuses despite the university obtaining an interdict.

UNIVERSITY OF KWAZULU-NATAL
#UKZNFeesMustFall first tweeted by @XManMnisi on 14 Oct, but on 14 Sept UKZN students at Westville barricade roads, calling for more funding. Cars are torched. Arrests. Westville SRC president, Lukhanyo 'Bhanda' Mtshingana, jailed for 30 days. UKZN students join #FeesMustFall protests on Wed, 21 Oct. March to ANC House on Fri, 23 Oct.

DURBAN UNIVERSITY OF TECHNOLOGY
#DUTFeesMustFall first tweeted on 20 Oct by @Khule101. Thousands of UKZN students join DUT students for a march to ANC House on Fri, 23 Oct, but DUT shuttle buses blocked by police, forcing students to push through blockades. Exams interrupted. Tyres set alight outside gates.

*No tweet data available for the University of the Western Cape

UNIVERSITY OF CAPE TOWN
#UCTFeesMustFall first tweeted on 14 Oct by @Uncle_JayB listing several universities. Protests begin after #RhodesMustFall says it will lead a protest on Mon, 19 Oct. UCT obtains court order against hashtags #UCTShutDown and #FeesMustFall. Ensuing protests steadily shut down campus, with exams postponed. UCT central to the march on parliament on Wed, 21 Oct, which sees 23 arrests and on-again off-again treason charges against #Bellville6.

KEY
Total tweets contributed by each university in the 30 days up to 24 Oct 2015.
Source: ROi Africa
First tweet data via ctrlq.org

LIMPOPO
GAUTENG
NORTH WEST
MPUMALANGA
FREE STATE
KWAZULU-NATAL
UFS 1.12%
NORTHERN CAPE
UKZN 0.67%
Central University of Technology 14.8%
UCT 23.59%
EASTERN CAPE
Walter Sisulu 0.55%
Fort Hare 2.79%
CPUT 0.89%
WESTERN CAPE
Nelson Mandela Metropolitan 2.93%
Stellenbosh 5.32%
Rhodes 7.4%

UNIVERSITY OF STELLENBOSCH
#StelliesFeesMustFall first tweeted on 12 Oct by @Feminist_Farai at SRC meeting. Following Open Stellenbosch protests against Afrikaans-language teaching, protests begin in earnest on Mon, 19 Oct, when students occupy the main administration building. Management obtains court order. A week of drama, with buildings occupied and renamed and two students arrested on Fri, 23 Oct.

NELSON MANDELA METROPOLITAN UNIVERSITY
#NMMUFeesMustFall first tweeted on 16 Oct by @lmtyobile. Protesting students rise against fees on Tues, 20 Oct, and later disrupt an awards ceremony. Students shut down NMMU and police use rubber bullets against them on Wed, 21 Oct. NMMU suspends classes on Fri, 23 Oct.

RHODES UNIVERSITY
#RhodesFeesMustFall first appears on Twitter on 14 Oct with @zee_xanga asking SRC when they will protest. #RUShutDown protests bring the university to a standstill on Mon, 19 Oct. Police step in at Midlands College after Rhodes students march there to shut down all tertiary education in Grahamstown.

UNIVERSITY OF FORT HARE
#FortHareFeesMustFall first tweeted 14 Oct by @fistvoices after reports of indebted students barred from exams. The same day sees #FortHareShutDown from @Athi_nangamso. Student threats begin Sat, 17 Oct. On Tues, 20 Oct, protests start. By Thurs, 22 Oct, students take control of Alice campus, set alight entrances. Exams postponed.

The moment also points us firmly in the direction of social justice. And #FeesMustFall is successful: President Jacob Zuma declares a moratorium on fee increases for 2016, but more importantly it successfully challenges a neoliberal shibboleth: that free tertiary education is unaffordable. As the students are stormed and tear-gassed at parliament, the rest of the nation rallies behind them and so do some big economic brains, who haul out their calculators.

It's clear that tuition costs at R22 billion a year are affordable by the fiscus if budget priorities are shifted. For the first time in many years, the scale of wasteful and corrupt expenditure is weighed up against a social need – students who want to study but can't afford to. Then, further budget debates are held: do we really need those new VIP presidential jets? Do we need to capitalise the BRICS Bank? The developing nations of Brazil, Russia, India and China, with South Africa, have started a bank and each agreed to fund it from their fiscuses. If we stopped wasting R30 billion a year on fruitless and wasteful expenditure (the auditor-general's last estimate), then we can afford to fund tertiary education.

The blooms of this Student Spring will allow us to ask a thousand questions about how money is spent and how priorities are set in South Africa – and allow the big questions on solidarity and social justice to take centre stage. The Student Spring offers, for me at least, a different way of understanding how we will complete our walk to freedom. The idea that whites are responsible for the hard limits of freedom recedes as the main theme, though the critique of privilege regularly takes on a racial hue.

And, finally, the politics of the moment breaks a pattern. South Africa is one-party dominant and political-party centric because of how our democracy has been established. Our political reporting has become equated with party political reporting when, in fact, the students reveal the more exciting possibilities in movements and offer lessons in cross-party solidarity in order to create a specific target of activism. South African civil society organised by the Treatment Action Campaign did it with the extension of antiretroviral drugs to a scaled mass of HIV-positive people; now students have done it with fees.

Many of the leaders of the Student Spring wore party political T-shirts, but they managed to work across and through these boundaries. As Nompendulo Mkhatshwa and Mcebo Dlamini addressed the ANC at Luthuli House, both wore party T-shirts but reflected none of the political sycophancy of older cadres that has come to hobble the party.

———

The students' movement will embolden the transformation initiative in other sectors as we saw happening in the midst of the student protest. They will show the adults. Here's an example how.

Silicotic. An awful word, but in October 2015 I begin to read it again and again to describe generations of mineworkers who are rendered disabled by the mine dust they inhaled as they liberated the gold from the hard seams of South African mines. Breathing in the dust causes a racking cough, weight loss and, often, disability. This is silicosis and if you have it, then you are silicotic. It is another of the morbid outcomes upon which South African mineral wealth is built. For decades, human rights lawyer Richard Spoor has laboured to use the courts to achieve compensation and justice for miners who are left in the lurch with miserable pensions and inadequate care.

In 2003, workers who contracted the lung disease asbestosis (which can lead to cancer) successfully sued Gencor. The quantum of damages was R465 million, which is held in trust by the Asbestos Relief Trust and the Kgalagadi Relief Trust. At the time of writing, the trusts had paid out R320 million to miners.

The silicosis case is likely to be much bigger. Silicosis is the disease arising from inhaling silica particles – described as acting like tiny blades on your lungs. They disable proper breathing and have been classified as carcinogenic.

Spoor has his sights on 32 gold-mining companies. The potential number of workers impacted is at 200 000 going back to 1965.

As we enter the era of a deepened social justice, the case is vital, so Spoor has lined up the great and the good to represent the miners. Except, they are almost all white – this is like rubbing salt in the wound of a country that is champing at the bit of whiteness and white supremacy. The racial arrangement of the advocates who will fight this landmark legal battle becomes a landmark of paternalism and it boils into the open, shattering the legal profession's tenuous unity. In the court, the black-owned advocates line up for the miners and the bosses: 40 of 42 are white. In 2015. Most of the instructing attorneys are also white men. In 2015.

Spoor writes: 'While the statistics are exaggerated, it is true that white men predominate in the legal profession …

'[But] why no black counsel on my team?

'The primary reason is that I use counsel willing to do the work at a reduced fee. That means counsel with an avowed and sincere commitment to public interest law. All our counsel are public interest lawyers …

'Secondly, we brief only exceptional counsel. By exceptional, I mean junior advocates who have graduated summa cum laude and who, quite frankly, border on genius. The seniors all rank among the top 20 advocates in the country. The number of black counsel who meet both these criteria is really small. Those who fit the bill were otherwise engaged when we needed them.

'Law is an elitist profession. My interest as the attorney is in winning the case and I have no latitude to accommodate unsuitable people. Colour does not qualify you if you don't meet other requirements. The work I do does not leave much room for charity or experimentation.'

This commentary goes down like the *Titanic*, sinking in its own miasma of prejudice, stereotype and paternalism. Spoor apologises but the cat is out of the bag.

Deputy Chief Justice Dikgang Moseneke responds a few days later as he delivers the Godfrey Pitje lecture: 'The dominant class dishes out patronage as it wishes and chooses. Briefing patterns of corporate work will always be reflective of [the] class, gender and race of the dominant decision makers. They are informed by both the financial interest and prejudices of the moneyed class. Often, all this boils down to the use of legal services of those with whom they share race, class and gender.'

Moseneke said this of the state's ability (and disability) to change the pattern because it was a massive consumer of legal services: 'All I hear is the state's monotonous demand for transformation of the profession and judiciary. Where would the race, class and gender diversity of the profession and bench come from when the state behaves as it does?' This was in reference to all levers of the state using white counsel ('opting for expediency' in his words) in its representations before the Constitutional Court.

Moseneke quoted Steve Biko's 'Black man, you are on your own' and said it may be time 'to go back to the professional trenches' to achieve needed change. The black legal profession is now back in the trenches. Thirteen top black advocates put out a joint statement saying: 'To suggest, as Mr Spoor does, that black advocates do not generally possess the skills, the commitment, the intelligence or ability of his white colleagues smacks of the Verwoerdian philosophy that most South Africans have long rejected.'

A few days later, the advocates requested and were allowed to address the court, which sat to begin hearing the silicosis cases. They made a trenchant speech to the dock on what Spoor's comments and what the composition of the legal teams said about South Africa and transformation.

It was unprecedented, as was the fact that the heads of the legal teams (all white) there distanced themselves from Spoor's comments and agreed there was a lot of work to be done to substantively transform the legal sector.

For advocate Roshnee Mansingh, the case symbolised the

following: 'If this case is to expose the prevailing run of play in the mining industry as the evidence in the case unfolds of a system of privilege for predominantly "white" capital and the neglect and outright exploitation of the black working class, it can be said that the first day of the proceedings have already exposed and proven another grim parallel fact: that the pattern of white privilege in the legal profession and the exclusion of black lawyers from mainstream legal practice remains firmly in place.'

As I continue to burrow and dig into South African race relations in the twenty-first century, Moseneke's categorisation of the private sector in general and the high legal profession in general as being run by a white dominant class gives me pause for thought. While I champ at the bit at suggestions that South Africa is anything but black-run, his speech reminds me and clarifies that there are different dominant classes.

If you put your ear to the ground, the entire private sector faces this same critique. Finance. Banking. Retail. Telecommunications. Mining. The ruling class here is different to the governing class of South Africa – it is regarded as run by a 'dominant class', in Moseneke's terms, that is white and totally out of kilter with the demands and precepts of the Constitution. This is unsustainable and is increasingly regarded as illegitimate if you look at the demographics of South Africa.

———

By the end of the process of writing this book, I have lost my arrogance and become curious again. Pat answers are no longer for me – though I feel that this is where South Africa can get stuck. The mantra of 'Oh, come on, just move on' is a hopeless failure. Equally, the mantra of believing that true freedom lies in having what whites have is a chimera and a path to disappointment and failure. The Student Spring poses tantalising and different potentials.

South Africa is given to apocalyptic scenarios. How long will South Africa survive? When Mandela goes (he's gone, sadly, and we are still here). The Tripartite Alliance is about to split (for 15 years now). Media freedom is imperiled (it could be regarded more highly, but journalists are not jailed or killed). The president wants a third term (we've had four presidents in 20 years – not one of whom has yet completed a second term). Pay back the money, or else! (or else, we will just keep saying it).

The first two scenarios are, to be honest, white concerns. But our history has made all of us into people who live on the edge and think in terms of black and white. Just like: what if there were no whites in South Africa?

The thing is, there are … whites and blacks. Colonialism should not have happened, but it did and so here we are – put into a state of coexistence at the foot of Africa to make of it what we will.

And, I would argue, we *have* made something of it. South Africa is not the state in concept alone – like Syria today or Afghanistan or Iraq or the Central African Republic. We are not at war, like Yemen or in the internecine war of the Democratic Republic of Congo. What do we do now?

The organisers of the event keep ringing to make sure I am on track as I am the responder. The room at the Gordon Institute of Business Science (GIBS) is almost booked out and the RSVPs keep pinging in. How long will South Africa survive? Lots of people want to hear scholar and writer R.W. (Bill) Johnson's answer.

I often visit the auditorium and have only a few times seen it this packed. It is a balmy evening in spring 2015. The birds are chirping as the days get longer. Jozi shrugs on her prettiest jacaranda blooms and cerise bougainvillea petals. It is perfect. The audience is not all white, as I had imagined it would be, though it is largely so. There are young black and Indian people too.

Here's what they heard.

What is now clear, just 20-odd years later and beyond any reasonable doubt, is that 'liberation' has failed, that the regime it has produced is quite incapable of governing South Africa as a free, democratic and functioning country. More and more things just don't work. This is not just rhetorical hyperbole. Around 80 percent of state schools don't work, and nor many state hospitals. The electricity supply has failed and the new power stations necessary to fill the gap are both many years late and many times more costly than they should have been – a sign of comprehensive management failure.

The civil service, the police and many of the local municipal bureaucracies clearly don't work. By July 2014 it was reported, for example, that every single municipality in the whole of North West province was bankrupt, victims of the usual ANC looting. There is a growing trade deficit but the government has decided to tax mineral exports. Similarly, the one great growth industry – tourism – stands to be throttled by ludicrous new immigration restrictions.

Throughout the economy the consequence of the disastrous failure of education is an ever-growing shortage of skilled labour of every kind yet the state's restrictions on the admission of skills professionals ensures that this cannot be met. As a rule of thumb, anything controlled or touched by the ANC – 'the liberation movement' – works very poorly or doesn't work at all.

On top of that, abuses of democracy pile one upon the other. Crime and insecurity rack the land, the economy fails, unemployment and inequality grow. The very integrity of the nation state is increasingly at stake. It is a commonplace to find people of all races who say things were better under apartheid.

Inevitably, some whites feel thus confirmed in their old contempt for all things African, but much sadder and more important is that this turn of events risks confirming many Africans in their lack of self-esteem, in their anxiety that the white supremacists might have been right after all. It is this agonized sense of threatened inferiority, almost of self-hatred, that lies behind many of the most passionate black panegyrics against whites. The worse the sense of failure, the more passionately the 'liberated' ego needs to vent itself. This is strictly Frantz Fanon territory. No one has written about it better. It is quite common among such outpourings to find anti-white racism, anti-Semitism, a hatred of

Asians, sexism, homophobia – every and any prop for desperately threatened egos.

This is the extract from his book, *How Long will South Africa Survive? The Looming Crisis*, which best answers Johnson's question: South Africa has not survived.

Does he or does he not speak for a large body of white opinion in our country? On that perfect evening in Johannesburg, a night, a time, a place, at such deep odds with his thesis about South Africa, the message resonates, I would say, with about half the room. The sense I get is that those who came are weighing things up. What *is* our future?

I see a different country; I may live in the same country but I experience an almost completely different one. I live in the country that helped make Trevor Noah, now executive producer and host of *The Daily Show*, the US's most popular comedic political satire. This child, of Swiss and Xhosa ancestry, makes jokes about growing up on Soweto's dusty streets, where he was nurtured by a loving gran.

Until he told his granny to stop talking to the media, she dragged out delicious baby snaps to give the media; snaps of a bright-eyed little boy grown on granny's love and mom's nurturing. His parents did not stay together for long; his mother was for years in an abusive and scalding relationship – hardships crafted him, as did an incessant drive and also a free country that provided a wonderful script for comedy and created opportunities for young people.

The night before the GIBS event to track whether South Africa

179

will survive or not, the country was glued to Comedy Central, the channel that broadcasts *The Daily Show*. Our Trevor Noah has taken the paramount seat at America's top-end comedy programme! For the week, the show's tune-ins from Johannesburg go stratospheric as we all celebrate this wonderful moment with a son made good.

So, coming off that high to probe 'How long will South Africa survive?', my questions are multifold. It's not the first time I have been at events like this where many in a majority white audience hold a bilious perspective on South Africa. If you choose to, you can see this South Africa because, God knows, some of it is true. If you choose to contemplate a different South Africa, you can see that too.

For 22 years now, I've honed the art of talent spotting – my part-time pleasure. I learnt to track and profile new establishments at the *Weekly Mail*, where, in the early nineties, editor Anton Harber got his staff to write the A to Z of politics to create an anatomy of the first democratic establishment.

From there, teams I've worked with have done the same with black business, women and young leading South Africans. There are entire new establishments of leaders and talents who are invested in and who have thrived in the new South Africa.

A few years ago, at *City Press*, we began to notice lots of people like Trevor Noah – cracking it big on the global stage. It turned into a publication called *100 World Class South Africans* – artists, business people, milliners, jewellers, performers all making global names.

Charlize Theron – Oscar-winning actress. Pretty Yende – opera singer. Whitey Basson – retail giant. Kirsten Goss – jeweller. Candice Swanepoel – lingerie model. Thebe Ikalafeng – Africa brands guru. John Kani – actor. William Kentridge – artist. Mary Sibande – artist. Fred Swaniker – schools founder.

Every year, we make a shortlist of 100 and have many more to add.

I ask Bill, as R.W. Johnson is known, what evidence he has for one of his key theses: that South Africa will inevitably need an International Monetary Fund bailout? While debt-to-GDP levels are growing uncomfortably, they are not close to bailout requirement. Business is, when I've met its representatives, confused by the ANC. Policy is a maze of uncertainty, but, on balance, some businesses have done well in the era of freedom.

Take my employer, Naspers. Unshackled in 1994, the company has found its wings, establishing a media behemoth at the top of global rankings. As I write, SABMiller is inking a deal with Brazilian bottler AB InBev, which had sought a merger. The buyout terms have the South African company's shareholding raising mighty cheers. Discovery is signing up hundreds of clients in China every day, its horizons extended and enabled by government's Look East policy that has seen South Africa become China's key partner on our continent. Shoprite is selling more champagne in a few stores in Nigeria than it does in all of South Africa.

When you get caught in the vortex of survival fear, then you will not see a single example of black agency – a factor missing almost completely from efforts such as Johnson's. It is a phenomenal accomplishment that South Africa has managed to extend a welfare net to 16.4 million people who get a grant of one sort or another. This has buoyed country and economy and is something we should be enormously proud of rather than miring it in the Thatcherite language that fears dependency rather than sees solidarity.

For every one thing, there is another. Johnson's book is a page-turner, especially when he applies his analytical mind to link all our everyday scandals and reveals a near-perfect system of patronage and corruption.

But, no credence is given to countervailing forces beginning to stack up against corruption. Public Protector Thuli Madonsela has become a counterweight and powerhouse. She represents a substantial body of opinion in society that is strongly opposed to corruption and which is steadily being organised into a movement against graft. There are others: a fabulous Constitutional Court; independent media; a strong and diverse civil society now likely to be led by students who are taking up issues outside of their immediate interests.

For every township school facing an exodus of pupils because of dysfunction and the debilitating impacts of a teachers' union that has failed freedom, there is a cheap, high-quality private school springing up. One of the quickest and under-reported trends is the advent of low-fee private schools catering for working-class and lower-middle-class pupils. Among these are Curro and SPARK schools, which, at scale, can fill the breach of a fragile public education system.

In 2015, BuzzFeed christened South Africa the most beautiful country in the world. Beautiful. To which I would add a few more descriptors. Interesting. Troubled. Fragile. Kind. Cruel. At just over 20 years old (in the sense of being free, equal, democratic), it is young and a work in progress with the potential to be made into something even more beautiful. That is, if we want to make it and not only watch it fall and fail. There is a substantial narrative, and it is largely but not only white, that is waiting for South Africa to fail. The next five years will separate out those with a pessimistic take and those of us who want our country to succeed.

EPILOGUE

I quickly learn what *Shaaaade* (Shade pronounced with a long 'a' to emphasise it) means in the language of social media and Twitter. It is the ultimate diss where you are embarrassed and put in your place in the sassiest way possible.

I get *Shaaaade* on the night of the Ruth First Memorial Lecture in August 2015; I see it after yoga when I scroll my timeline to see what I have missed. I search the hashtag on Twitter. I tend to go every year so interesting has the annual affair run by Wits become. This year, my commitment to getting right my downward-facing dog (a core yoga pose) had found me taking a class instead. When I see what happened at the lecture, I thank the gods of yoga for ensuring I hadn't been in the Wits Great Hall.

By the time I get to it, Twitter is ablaze about the lecture – it has trended and the black womanhood is overjoyed and owns my timeline. Sisonke Msimang and Panashe Chigumadzi have set the place on fire (metaphorically, the real fire would come later in the year) – the latter with an empassioned appropriation of the concept and exposition of the pain of the coconut, the term that has come to describe a generation of young black people who grew up in suburbia and developed accents and other cultures of the suburbs.

Sisonke has worked to the topic of whether black and white

people can be friends. For the longest time, writers (including me) have propagated the need for a Steve Biko for the twenty-first century. This is because 2015 has been a year punctuated by racist incidents and attacks – race consciousness is higher than I have ever seen it, and race relations are at their lowest ebb.

Sisonke had become that voice for me – navigating beautifully the story of our times and writing essays so presciently that she puts her finger on the pulse of what is eating us. So, I am devastated that I have come up for sisterly excoriation by her and the people's poet Lebo Mashile in their brilliant performance of Sisonke's research. This is for my self-confessed impatience with South Africa's race talk. I once wrote that if I encountered racism, I had the agency to kick it away like tumbleweed. And I surprise, I think, another hero, Achille Mbembe, by decrying that our young people are not a little more ... shall we call it ... Chinese, in their chase for entrepreneurship and market share.

Sisonke and Lebo are sheroes to me; Achille is philosopher-king, so to find myself outside their circle of approval is disorientating in the extreme – as if you are that kid cast aside from the popular circle and made to take your place with the outcasts. I want to run away and hide. I am indeed in the shade.

But the vulnerability it provokes is good for it forces me to listen and to hear, to search beyond my platitudes for what I believe in. It ejects me from my comfort zone and ensures I do not become part of the self-satisfied elite, impatient that others simply do not get it. What is it I think about race and freedom? What should I be thinking?

———

Ever since I read Frederick Douglass's essay 'What to the Slave is the Fourth of July?' I have been enamoured by him. Douglass was a famed abolitionist and had spent his early life as a slave in various horrific servitudes. He taught himself to read and later escaped north to become one of the United States's great orators and a leading abolitionist.

The essay is a speech he delivered to a liberal ladies' club, when he posed the great question and then answered it: the fourth of July means very little to the slave for he or she is deprived of the liberty at the heart of American independence. He later edited and owned *The North Star*, one of the pioneers of the US's black press.

In Washington D.C. in mid-2015, I carve out time to head onto the Black Heritage Trail and find Douglass's house, Cedar Hill, which has been turned into a museum. It is fascinating and I can't tear myself away from the riveting story of his life and his bravery. Douglass spent his last years in this regal home, as a statesman and community leader at the centre of public life. He read, debated, lifted weights (I saw them), entertained and loved (Douglass's first wife, disabled by illness, stayed in the house together with his second wife).

His story resonates with me and that bit of historic tourism was one of my highlights. South Africa asks the same question. What to the enfranchised is democracy worth? What does Freedom Day, the 27th of April, mean if you are still in struggle and in a situation that has not changed adequately?

And, later, I realise that bootstrap stories like Douglass's always have my undivided attention because of my own story.

Of course, I did not grow up in chains (although it felt that way sometimes) but I am a bootstraps person. When I clicked at about five years old onto the extent of the injury of our apartness, I plotted ways to get out of it. To be free, I worked from as soon as possible and hustled for every opportunity – a trait and theme that has seeped into my work and been picked apart by Sisonke and Achille.

But it is my template, and not one you can impose on a country, especially ours, which is far more Scandinavian in its outlook – the South African narrative supports social solidarity and the idea of the state, and not the individual, as the agent of change. The mantra of the state is to amend the Biko metaphor to 'black man, you are *not* on your own', or you should not be.

But there is something else in the story of Frederick Douglass that also informs my view, and that is a story of absolute black agency – of what you can do with freedom. It is an idea that, truth be told, I find undervalued in our public deliberations.

This absence too often allows a wasteful, bloated and increasingly venal political order to cover its inefficiency and absence of care and love in the language of race-blaming.

The large and economically powerful state does not use its black agency to secure a better life for more.

During the October 2015 students' uprising, it is this idea of what a mass of black-led students of all stripes can do that is inspiring – that they have agency to change a massive superstructural idea (that education cannot be free), and it is deeply compelling.

——

My lodestars have always been non-racialism and non-sexism – creeds I now find so far out of vogue that, even while they are constitutional principles, they enjoy little cachet in society. And what do they even mean?

Why do they enjoy so little traction? For one, the principles are poorly understood and so easily hijacked by conservative elements that use them as evidence of the need to move on without doing the hard work. And there is tremendous equity in blackness – for so long imprisoned by the varied tortures of colonialism and then apartheid, the spirit of non-racialism, which seeks to erase race as a key determinant, there is an entire generation (and more) for whom the philosophy is a total non-starter.

For a humanist, this is hard to acknowledge, but then to declare oneself a humanist learning the spirit of Ubuntu risks equal derision. No matter, it is where I find myself to raise these concepts. It is out of place: in majority white audiences, the understanding thereof is too glib. In majority black audiences, I get the firm sense of people thinking, 'Are you kidding, lady?'

After the process of writing, it is a lonely place but one in which I find significant comfort. There is too much racism and incipient racial superiority not to declare yourself anti-racist too.

But I have found there are really clever people thinking us out of our dilemmas – they are using old sages to help us find a path. Xolela Mangcu in his edited collection *The Colour of our Future* cites Steve Biko thus: 'I would suggest that a race transcendant leader is one who makes it possible for people of different racial groups to work together for a common purpose, grounded in what Biko called a "joint culture". Race transcendent leadership is not to be confused with the concept of post-racialism that has come in the wake of Barack Obama's election in the United States, or the concept of "Post-Blackness" ... As an alternative [to non-racialism], Biko suggested an anti-racist integration based on mutual respect for each other's cultures – the concept of "joint culture".'

This is, to me, a useful new lodestar to strive towards, as is this retrospective by Joel Netshitenzhe, the executive director of the Mapungubwe Institute for Strategic Reflection, who writes in the same book: 'Unique in the 1994 settlement was an acceptance on the part of the leadership of the majority that there would be an orderly transition and a process of transformation based on legitimate legality; that transformation would not entail grabbing from whites even the material privileges illegitimately accumulated under apartheid ... in the same vein, it was expected of the white community to reciprocate with ... a commitment actively to contribute to righting the historical injustice.

'The question is whether there is substantive progress and whether power relations are changing. This also raises the issue of a mindset among black people to defy the constraints of an oppressive legacy. In this regard, Touré (citing Michael Eric Dyson) poses a critical question about the danger of self-limitation on the part of black people: "The moment we shatter those artificial encumbrances of race – a stereotype from without or rigid archetype from within – and feel no need to respond to either is the moment we are vastly improved, profoundly human and therefore become the best Black people we can become."'

I came to write this book because I found the black adherence to theories of whiteness self-limiting. And, so, the question: what if there were no whites in South Africa? To which I got the answer: it is not about whites, but about whiteness – the system of privilege and prejudice that is still held to be in place.

I get some of that, but my question remains: what is it that black South Africans want to do with this fine land of ours? Does an obsession with whites and whiteness not obstruct the building to be done?

———

Some of my best friends are wh—

No, I'm not going to do that. Until First National Bank did away with the need to go into a bricks-and-mortar bank, there were two ladies who stood outside my Rosebank branch collecting for an orphanage or some other charity. They held collection letters. Once, years ago, when I did not have change, I heard one lady tell the other that Indians never give.

Scalded by the stereotype, I spent years and lots of money trying to disprove their view of me by stuffing notes into their hands whenever I went by. Any discussion that includes the phrase 'the whites' or 'the blacks' is likely to include broad and gross generalisations about one another, and I've deliberately tried to steer clear of it – although this kind of talk romps wildly across our national narrative.

But on the other side, I started this book listing my various collisions with white privilege. An update: my colleagues and I worked well together for many years at the *Mail & Guardian*, even though they initially had thought I could not cut it. We had hard discussions through the years and when I left, I received the kindest note.

My neighbour, who called me Muriel for years, got it right. In the course of writing this book, I got a note about building works at his house and he spelt my name correctly. Yay!

My workplace has been a source of growth and empowerment that I am deeply grateful for and aware of.

My experience of our country and of reporting on it for almost a quarter of a century is that every time you think you have hit upon a certainty about a person or a group, they will surprise you. It's not a particularly national condition, but it's a decidedly human one.

But I also experience this time as more race-in-your-face than I have known it, so Netshitenzhe's philosophical path is appealing. He speaks of '… an approach that acknowledges, but is not limited by, race. In this first instance, it transcends the syndrome of negatives, as in "non-racial", "non-sexist" and so on; secondly, it poses as the ultimate objective a purpose more enduring than the pursuit of racial equality.'

He continues: 'Firstly, not being limited by race does not and should not suggest the post-racial notion that "race does not exist or that we are somehow beyond race" – a form of colour blindness. Secondly, emphasizing an overarching identity rooted in South African-ness does not and should not imply that South African society would become a melting pot of undifferentiated beings. From sport and music preferences, to language, ethnic origins, religious beliefs, and so on, individuals will continue to evince and take pride in their multiple identities.'

Netshitenzhe raises a question vital for our white compatriots, especially those who control the levers of economic power. Has the founding compact to right the historical injustice been achieved? We have peace. But is it sufficient?

And is it possible to right those historic injustices without making anybody feel like a second-class citizen who does not enjoy the full spectrum of rights and responsibilities that our Constitution grants to each of us?

The students held, for me, the potential to see us out of our interregnum – that period of limbo between that which is struggling to die and that which is yet to be born. And this phrase from Mandela stayed with me through the writing: 'It always seems impossible until it is done.'

SELECTED REFERENCES

Books

Bradford, Sarah. *Harriet Tubman: The Moses of Her People* (New York: Dover Publications, 2004).

Cargill, Jenny. *Trick or Treat: Rethinking Black Economic Empowerment* (Johannesburg: Jacana, 2010).

Douglass, Frederick. *Narrative of the Life of Frederick Douglass: An American Slave* (Cambridge, MA: Harvard University Press, 2009).

Johnson, R.W. *How Long Will South Africa Survive: The Looming Crisis* (Johannesburg and Cape Town: Jonathan Ball, 2015).

Mangcu, Xolela (editor). *The Colour of our Future: Does Race Matter in Post-apartheid South Africa?* (Johannesburg: Wits University Press, 2015).

Sparks, Allister. *Tomorrow Is Another Country* (Cape Town: Struik, 1994).

Documents

Census 2011: Census in Brief (Statistics South Africa)

Commission for Employment Equity Annual Report, 2013–2014 (Department of Labour)

South Africa Survey, 2014–2015 (South African Institute of Race Relations)

South African Reconciliation Barometer, 2011–2014 (Institute for Justice and Reconciliation)

State Land Audit (Chief Surveyor-General, 2013)

Who Are the Middle Class in South Africa? Does it Matter for Policy? (Justin Visagie, Econ3x3, 29 April 2013)

Ferial Haffajee

Newspapers
Business Day (various)

City Press (various)

Financial Mail (25 June–1 July 2015)

Sowetan (various)

The Times (various)

Round tables
Three round-table discussions were held in the course of 2015.
Discussants included:

Danielle Bowler: researcher, feminist, artist

Ziyana Lategan: student

Gugulethu Mhlungu: editor at *City Press* and broadcaster on Talk
Radio 702

Andile Mngxitama: activist, scholar and former MP

Tiyani Rikhotso: spokesperson, Department of Transport

Khusela Sangoni: spokesperson, African National Congress
headquarters

Melissa Steyn: professor and director of Wits Centre for Diversity
Studies

Mayihlome Tshwete: spokesperson, Department of Home Affairs

ACKNOWLEDGEMENTS

People have spluttered: 'You wrote it while working?' I could not have done so without researcher Verashni Pillay who, with her exacting eye, industriousness and depth helped me with the material in order to put this book together. She asked me tough questions and gave me great advice. Thank you, Verashni. And I'm so happy you have taken that top perch at the beloved *Mail & Guardian*. Enjoy it.

I am deeply grateful for the thinkers and activists for a better South Africa who gave so generously of their time and their ideas at the round tables held to understand the narrative at the core of this book: Danielle Bowler, Ziyana Lategan, Gugulethu Mhlungu, Andile Mngxitama, Tiyani Rikhotso, Khusela Sangoni, Melissa Steyn and Mayihlome Tshwete. I have learnt so much from you and changed my tune in varied ways.

Thank you, Babalwa Nyembezi, for thinking through this project with me at the outset and being a fresh young voice on a tough manuscript. Thank you, Sally Hines, for your sensitive editing, fact checking and prescient questions.

To *City Press*. I am because you are. All of you have taught me what I know of Mzansi and race and then some. Your work is threaded through this book and I am grateful for your talents, curiosity, frankness and kindness. Masehume Motloenya, your kind assistance from top to toe in this writing project has been invaluable. Thank you Johannes Mailula for helping me drop and fetch so many things.

Our award-winning graphics team at Graphics24 has taught me to tell stories in engaging and interesting ways. I am grateful for their permission to use some of this work in this book.

Andrea Nattrass, thank you for coaxing a book out of me – I have enjoyed it so much there may be another one in me. The joy of writing more than 140 characters and 700 words has emboldened my pen and heightened my sense of curiosity.